Elizabeth Rundle Charles

Te Deum Laudamus

Christian Life in Song the Song and the Singers

Elizabeth Rundle Charles

Te Deum Laudamus
Christian Life in Song the Song and the Singers

ISBN/EAN: 9783337181192

Printed in Europe, USA, Canada, Australia, Japan

Cover: Foto ©Lupo / pixelio.de

More available books at **www.hansebooks.com**

Te Deum Laudamus

CHRISTIAN LIFE IN SONG

The Song and the Singers

BY THE LATE

MRS. RUNDLE CHARLES

AUTHOR OF "CHRONICLES OF THE SCHÖNBERG-COTTA FAMILY," ETC.

"The Holy Church throughout all the world doth acknowledge Thee."

FIFTH EDITION, REVISED AND ENLARGED

SOCIETY FOR PROMOTING CHRISTIAN KNOWLEDGE,
LONDON: NORTHUMBERLAND AVENUE, W.C.;
43, QUEEN VICTORIA STREET, E.C.
BRIGHTON: 129, NORTH STREET.
NEW YORK: E. & J. B. YOUNG & CO.

1897

PUBLISHED UNDER THE DIRECTION OF THE TRACT COMMITTEE

PREFACE

(TO FIRST AND SECOND EDITIONS)

THE translations in the following pages are all new, unless when the contrary is stated; because, the object of the translator being rather historical than literary, it was more essential than in ordinary cases that the colouring of the present should not be thrown over the faith of the past. The first aim, therefore, has been to represent faithfully the creed of the hymn-writers; the next, to reproduce their thoughts and images. Wherever it has been found practicable, the original metres have been imitated.

It is hoped that this volume will explain its own purpose; and it therefore only remains to state the authorities on which the hymns and biographies are given.

The historical facts are drawn from the ordinary histories and biographies, German, French, and English.

The Oriental, Ambrosian, and Mediæval hymns

have been selected and translated from those in Daniel's "Thesaurus Hymnologicus," Mone's "Hymni Latini Medii Ævi," and Trench's "Sacred Latin Poetry." The hymns of Ephrem Syrus have been re-translated from the German version of the Syriac given in Daniel's "Thesaurus;" all the rest have been rendered from the original languages, and are commended to the charity of those whose greater familiarity with classical literature may detect blemishes unperceived by the translator.

The German hymns have been translated from Dr. Leopold Pasig's edition of Luther's "Geistliche Lieder," Albrecht Knapp's "Liederschatz," and a "Sammlung von Kirchenliedern aus dem Gesangbuche der evangelischen Brüdergemeinden;" the Swedish, from hymns kindly sent to the writer by Swedish friends.

If the Christian men of former times cannot be our perfect examples, since we and they may own but One, they are still our fathers; and their creed, although not our Bible, is nevertheless our precious and sacred heritage. It is trusted that the treasures of sacred song, faintly reflected in these translations, may serve to illustrate that unity of faith which binds one age to another through the Communion of Saints. If they help to raise any hearts to Him in whom alone that unity is life, the first and dearest purpose of the writer will be attained.

London, 1858.

PREFACE

(TO FOURTH EDITION)

THE subject of Hymns and Hymn-writers has been so much studied, and hymns themselves have taken so much larger a place in our literature and in the public services of our Churches, during the thirty years which have elapsed since these pages were written, that for some time the author thought it unnecessary to republish this volume. But as it seems thought by some whose opinion has weight that the little book has an individuality of its own which nothing else precisely replaces, it is offered again to those who may care for it.

Some omissions have been made of criticisms on various imperfections and perversions, in order to fulfil more harmoniously the object of the whole, which was positive and not negative, to bring into light not the mistakes and exaggerations which in all ages have tended to choke or to discolour the fountains of truth, but the living water of Christian life itself in hymns and hearts.

PREFACE

(TO FIFTH EDITION)

THIS Edition has been revised and enlarged especially with a view to making it a companion volume to "*Ecce Homo, Ecce Rex*," "The Fruits of Christian Life in Works of Mercy," and "The Voice of Christian Life in Song."

NOTE OF EDITOR, S.P.C.K.

MRS. CHARLES was at work upon this volume up to a few days before her death. She regarded it as the last of her literary labours. The title "Te Deum Laudamus," chosen by herself, appropriately expresses the joy of one about to enter upon her rest, after a long life spent in the service of her Master.

The sheets of the work had unfortunately not the advantage of her final revision, and a few blemishes may therefore be discovered in the volume.

October 1897.

CONTENTS

CHAP.		PAGE
I.	HYMNS OF THE BIBLE	11
II.	THE "TERSANCTUS," THE "GLORIA IN EXCELSIS," AND THE "TE DEUM"	23
III.	THE ANONYMOUS GREEK HYMNS	33
IV.	CLEMENT OF ALEXANDRIA, EPHREM SYRUS, AND GREGORY OF NAZIANZUM	47
V.	ST. AMBROSE AND THE AMBROSIAN HYMNS	82
VI.	GREGORY THE GREAT, VENANTIUS FORTUNATUS, AND THE VENERABLE BEDE	128
VII.	ST. BERNARD	162
VIII.	MEDIÆVAL HYMNS	184
IX.	THE HYMNS OF GERMANY	223
X.	HYMNS OF SWEDEN AND OTHER COUNTRIES	254
XI.	ENGLISH HYMNS	267
XII.	CONCLUSION	301

CHRISTIAN LIFE IN SONG

CHAPTER I

HYMNS OF THE BIBLE

F Church history is to be anything different from secular history, it should surely be the record of Christian truth, speaking through the lives of Christian men; the story of the struggle between selfishness and Divine love, of the Life which has pierced through and outlived the corruption and decay of States; the echo of the accents of truth and love, penetrating, like a musical tone, through the market-din and battle-tumult of the world. But, too often, how different is the fact! With what a weariness of disappointment we turn from pages which seem but the transferring of the old, selfish, secular ambitions to a new arena; the name of truth, and even of God, being merely the weapon of the strife, whilst Self is the god whose glory is contended for!

Yet we are sure, since the Prince of life arose from the tomb, the life of Christianity has never been altogether buried again; and to watch for it, and rejoice in it when found, seem among the chief objects for which Church history is worth being studied.

And as we watch, much is revealed to us. We trace Christian life through its various manifestations of love, and find the golden chain unbroken through the ages, however dim at times the gold may shine. It manifests itself in its expansive form of love to man, in countless works of mercy, in missions, and hospitals, and ransomings of captives, and individual acts of love and self-sacrifice which cannot be numbered. We trace it in its direct manifestation of love to God, in martyrdoms, and in hymns; the yielding up of the life to death for truth, and the breathing out of the soul to God in song.

The object of these pages is to follow the last track, by listening to the voice of that stream of spiritual song which has never been altogether silent on earth; by attempting to reproduce some notes of the song, and some likeness of the singers.

And may not such a search have its peculiar use, in a day and a land like ours? It is, no doubt, difficult to ascertain the true characteristics of the nation or the times we live amongst; partly because we are too near to make the perspective correct, and partly because the atmosphere which colours the scene also colours our own minds. The rumble of the highway we are treading overpowers the roar of the retreating thunder-storm; the riot of to-day sounds louder than the revolution of the last century; and thus age after age has seemed to hear in its own tumults the echo of those chariot-wheels which are still long in coming.

Yet some of the characteristics of the sea we are sailing on we must know, for safety, if not for science. Would it not, for instance, be generally admitted, that the character of Christian life, in our own time, is rather humane than devotional, its tendency rather outward than upward, its utterance rather in works of mercy than in songs of praise? Have we not all to be especially on our guard that we do not make our worship merely public service, and so fail to make our service worship? In our own free age and country, when opportunities for doing good are so multiplied, when there is not a talent or a grace but may find its own full and appropriate exercise in the great field of work, may we not learn something from the men of those more fettered days, when Christian life, hemmed in on all sides but one, rose with all its force towards the heavens from which no human tyranny could shut it out? And thus may we not learn more to seek communion with God, not merely as the strength for work, but as the end and crown of all work; not only as the means of life, but as its highest object?

Not, indeed, that active and contemplative piety are opposed to each other. Martha's service would have been more efficient had it been less cumbered, had she listened as well as served. Mary, when the time came, could anoint the feet, at which she had loved to sit, with ointment whose perfume filled the house. And those who serve God best of all are those who "see His face."

Nor in these busy times of ours has the service of song ceased on earth; the melody in the heart flows on still, and gushes forth in music; and it is not of an extinct species that we think when we search out those old hymns. The accents of the first singers are no dead language to us, and their life is ours. The first hymn recorded in the Bible is also the last: the song chanted first on the shores of the Red Sea, echoes back to us from the "sea of glass mingled with fire."

Of the mode of worship in the old patriarchal times, we know little; but, surely, music was not only heard in the city of Cain. Earth can never have been without her song to God. The first wave of promise which flowed in to cover the first wave of sin, must have found its response in the heart of man; but after the first universal hymn of Eden was broken, and the music of creation fell into a minor, whilst the wail of human sin and sorrow ran across all its harmonies, a long silence reigns in the hymn-book of the Church universal; and through all the records of violence and judgment, from the flood and the ark, from patriarchal tent and Egyptian kingdom, the only song which has reached us is the wail of a murderer echoing the curse of Cain.

We read of altar and sacrifice, of meditations in the fields at eventide, of visions, and prayers, and accepted intercessions, and we feel sure that those who walked in the light, like Enoch or Abraham, must have had their hearts kindled into music. But from the green earth rising out of the flood; from the shadow of the great oak at Mamre; from the fountains and valleys and upland pastures of the Promised Land, where the tents of the patriarchs rose amidst their flocks; from the prisons and palaces of Egypt, we catch no sound of sacred song. So far the stream flows for us underground.

The first recorded hymn in the Bible is the utterance of the national thanksgiving of Israel by the Red Sea. When the Church becomes visible, her voice becomes audible.

The waves flowed back to their ancient tide-marks, the pathway through the sea was hidden for ever, and, with it, the hosts of the enemies of God and of Israel. The way of escape had become the wall of demarcation, and looking back on that sea, with all its buried secrets, above its ripple and its roar the song burst from the lips of Moses and the children of Israel.

It was a type of all the psalms which have been sung on earth since. It was a song of victory. It was a song of redemption. It was "sung to the Lord." The silence of the dead was beneath that sea, the silence of the desert was around it, and there first it is written that the Song of Redemption pierced through the long wail of the Fall. There the first notes of that great chant of victory were chanted which echo along the crystal sea, far, far beyond our hearing, into the depths of eternity.

That song has never ceased since on this earth. One dying voice has carried on its accents to another. From time to time it bursts on our ears in a chorus of triumph; at times, even Elijah can hear no voice but his own. But God has heard it ceaselessly, we may not doubt; and while some tones, loud and musical in man's ears, have failed to pierce beyond the atmosphere of earth, countless melodies, inaudible to us, have reached his ear, and been welcomed by His love.

Among the many books which God has caused to be written for us to make up His One Book—family records, royal chronicles, histories of the past and future, proverb and prophecy—we have one book which speaks not so much to man from God as to God for man. In the Book of Psalms the third person of the historical narratives, the "Thus saith the Lord" of the Law and the Prophets, is exchanged for the supplicating or rejoicing "O Lord, my God," "Unto Thee, O Lord, will I sing." Beginning often in the tumultuous depths, these psalms soar into the calm light of heaven. An inspired liturgy for all time and the prophetic utterance of the sacrificial sorrow which has redeemed the world, they are yet the spontaneous natural expression of the conflicts and hopes, the repentings and thanksgivings of the human hearts which first uttered them.

Whatever criticism ("higher" or "lower") may discover as to the fountains from which this or that part of the river came, it is one mighty ancient river, from fountains ever fresh. Variety of authorship is indeed one of its essential characteristics. Like all the true Hymnals of the Church Militant its songs are battle songs; the psalms of David at all events were not spun out in leisurely literary retirement, but amidst the struggles of a most active and eventful life. Amongst the flocks he led by the "green pastures and still waters" in his peaceful but daring youth, his heart turned to the Lord his Shepherd; from the rocks and mountain fortresses amongst which he had taken refuge from Saul, he called on the Lord his Fortress and his high Tower; awaking in anguish from the madness of his great crime, he uttered those self-despairing yet most trustful words on which the sighs of repentant sinners have taken wing to God during thousands of years. It cannot be without purpose that so much is revealed to us of the life of the "Sweet Singer of Israel;" otherwise we might have thought that sighs only, not songs, became the penitent, however freely the "much is forgiven;" and then many a vase of precious perfume might have been held back in shame, and we might have missed the truth that the deepest music of the Church is often mingled with her penitential tears. "For the hearts of a hundred men strove and struggled together within the narrow continent of that single heart."[1]

There is one characteristic of this ancient psalmody sometimes lacking in the hymns of later days: "The sound of a host is in them, the power of a great corporate life, a passionate patriotism, sometimes indeed throbbing with the avenging fierceness of the national life which inspired it, but with all their intense individuality these grand psalms never sink into feeble wails over the weariness of the way, or into other worldly clamours for selfish escape

[1] Irving, quoted in Stanley's "Jewish Church."

and satisfaction." The deliverances they crave are for all the oppressed and wronged; the king they welcome is the king who "judges the poor, saves the children of the needy, and breaks in pieces the oppressor." The God they appeal to is the God who is the helper of the friendless, who beholdeth ungodliness and wrong. The moral and the spiritual are not separated; in them the sins against which they flash into indignation are no mere spiritual declensions or ceremonial inaccuracies but plain, commonplace, or hideous undeniable crimes—injustice, unmercifulness, extortion, heaping up riches by oppression, persecuting the poor helpless man, not "setting the mind to do good."

The music of all nature moreover is gathered into these wonderful psalms. The order and beauty of the starry heavens, "valleys standing so thick with corn that they laugh and sing," the trees of the field that clap their hands, the birds that sing among their branches, the voice of seas and floods, the rivers that run among the hills, the beasts of the fields that quench their thirst at them, the young ravens that cry, the swallows that build their nests unforbidden in the temple. And at moments the old Hebrew songs soar, by the very loftiness of their communion with God, to the infinite breadth of His compassions, rising above the highest mere national hopes to the joyful adoration of all lands, the righteous governing of all nations. Throughout the ages the grand sacred song rolls on, gathering in depth and volume from prophet to prophet, yet always with the same ideals—the relief of the oppressed, the redressing of wrongs, the drawing out the soul to the hungry, liberty to the captives, binding up the broken-hearted, beauty and joy springing from the triumph of goodness and truth. Ever deeper also and nearer draws the double strain of the new song of self-sacrifice and redemption of the "Man of Sorrows" who was to heal all sorrows, and fill all the waste places of the earth with song of everlasting joy; until at last the "Glad tidings of great joy" came audibly to earth as the song of the angels broke on the ears of the shepherds keeping watch over their flocks by night.

The first recorded Jewish hymn was chanted by the great lawgiver, with a nation for his chorus. The first Christian hymn was sung by Mary the mother of Jesus, with no audience, as far as we know, but one other faithful woman. The contrast, doubtless, has its meaning. Her song, like the ancient Psalms of her people, full as it is of her own transcendent joy, extends to the deliverance and joy of all—the filling of the hungry, the exaltation of the meek, the putting down of the proud. And yet her hymn is no angelic song, no thanksgiving of a spirit looking on adoring from the outside at the great miracle of Divine love. That human tone, which gives its deepest music to the new song of heaven, is not wanting in Mary's. She can say, "My Saviour," that she also may sing hereafter, "Thou wast slain, and hast redeemed us by Thy blood!" The Magnificat of the blessed Virgin is but another strain in the great Song of Redemption.

Then Zacharias, when the seal is taken off his lips, and his mouth is opened to praise God, at once his heart is borne away beyond his own special blessing, on the great tide of joy, which is the common element of all the redeemed, and the natal hymn of the Baptist soars away into a Christmas carol. For a moment his song alights on the peculiar gladness which had visited his house, the child of his old age, who was to be the prophet of the Highest; but then again it soars upward, until it is lost in the early beams of the Dayspring from on high.

One other hymn completes that first cluster; and this, unlike the other two, was uttered in the Temple. It may have been long indeed since any fire from heaven had touched the mercenary sacrifices there, or any gush of fresh inspiration had pierced the icy routine of the services. At length, however, the heavens, which had seemed so impenetrable, opened, and before the veil was rent, and they melted away for ever, service and sacrifice shone with a new and divine radiance from the Sun which was rising behind them.

Once more the music of inspired song was heard in the Temple; not from the choir of David's priestly singers, but from the lips of an old man, as he held the infant Saviour in his arms. Yet, in the few simple words with which Simeon welcomed the joy he had waited for so long, he rose to a height at which even Pentecostal gifts did not always sustain apostles. The old man's vision reached to the universal promise; and he saw in Jesus not only the Glory of Israel, but the Light to lighten the Gentiles. With such a vision well might he depart in peace!

Thus the first triad of Christian hymns (the three matin-songs of Christianity) was completed. Ere another was added to the sacred list, the great victory which had been thus sung had to be won; not with songs, but with strong crying, and tears, and unutterable anguish. To human ears the completion of the great victory was announced, not with shouts of triumph and songs of angelic hosts, but by one dying human Voice, speaking in darkness from the Cross.

"*When Jesus therefore had received the vinegar, he said, It is finished: and he bowed his head, and gave up the ghost.*"

Yet are not those dying words the fountain-head of every hymn of joy and triumph which men have ever sung since Eden was closed, or ever will sing, throughout eternity?

The Bible records the words of but one other hymn; for a hymn it was, whether said or sung.

The Son of God had burst the bands of the grave, and had ascended to be where He is now, at the right hand of God; and, as He promised, the Comforter had come, and, knit together in living unity by Him, the Church had appeared a living temple of God in the world. Thus the only hymn recorded in the Acts is not, like those in the Gospels, sung by solitary voices. It is a choral burst of praise; and, like so many since, it is struck from the heart of the Church by the hand of persecution. The first persecution of the Church gave birth to her first hymn. Peter and John came back from their night in prison to the band of believers; and they lifted up their voices to God with one accord, and the place where they met was shaken, as if by an earthquake.

After that we have no record of any hymn (unless the thirteenth chapter of first Corinthians, rising sublime and detached, as it does, from the general level of the epistle, may be called one) until the songs of heaven fall on our hearts from the heights of the Apocalyptic vision. Then from within the gates of pearl, from the city which is also a paradise, from beside the fountain of life, and from before the throne of God and the Lamb, we catch the tones of the new song, and find it the ever new Song of Redemption, the psalm of the new creation; the song which Moses sang, and David, and Hannah, and Mary the mother of Jesus, and the early Church, when she first tasted the bitter cup of her Lord; the song which every sinner that repenteth sings, and the angels echo; which we are still singing, and still learning now, and which will be new in its inexhaustible depths of joy for ever and ever.

CHAPTER II

THE "TERSANCTUS," THE "GLORIA IN EXCELSIS," AND THE "TE DEUM"

THREE Hymns and two Creeds have come down to us from early times, and have been incorporated into our daily services, besides the hymn preserved in our Ordination Services. They have descended to us pure and distinct, through the gradually thickening corruptions of many centuries. Fragments of the language of heaven, often preserved by those who knew not the interpretation, they must, through those dark and confused ages, have formed channels of communication with God for many a perplexed but believing heart.

In the preservation of the Holy Scriptures themselves, through similar perils, we recognize with adoration the controlling hand of God; and we may surely also attribute it to His merciful providence, that through those centuries, when so many would receive no spiritual food except through the external Church, and the authorities of the Church (by the testimony of their own adherents) so often gave the stone, if not the serpent, to her children, instead of bread, her daily Offices should have been kept so pure, enshrining in their midst the Apostles' and the Nicene Creeds, the two Hymns now in our Communion Service, and the " Te Deum."

The preservation of the Creeds is, however, scarcely so remarkable as that of the Hymns. That the Creeds should ever have become what they are, is indeed more wonderful than that once formed they should have remained intact.

That out of the fierce word-battles of the Oriental Churches, when eternal truths were made the subject of courtly intrigue and popular tumult, and the populace of Greek and Syrian cities were ready to shed each other's blood on account of the relations of the Persons in the Trinity to one another, meanwhile concerning themselves very little about their own relations to God; when there was danger of an abstract Trinity in Unity being worshipped instead of the living and redeeming God; that from such fierce and passionate controversies those first simple and living Creeds should have been evolved, is indeed wonderful. And since the formation of the Creeds was no new revelation, the fact may surely teach us a comforting lesson in ecclesiastical history. Living words cannot proceed from lifeless souls; and the ages which compacted the Creeds, must surely, beneath that tumult of noisy controversies and strife "who should be greatest," whose echoes, as they reach us, we are apt to call Church history, have borne to heaven many a cry of true prayer, and many a soft chorus of thanksgiving. As St.

Augustine said,[1] "We look on the surface and see only the scum; beneath we should find the oil."

Thus the Creeds are witnesses not only for the truth they utter, but for the Church which uttered them. Once formed, however, the great difficulty as regarded them was over. They were sealed with all the authority of Church and State; they were systematic documents with sharply-defined edges; they were fenced in with anathemas, and the anathemas were fortified with civil penalties. The subtle and tumultuous, yet servile populace, who entered into doctrinal controversies with the eagerness with which their forefathers had contended for political rights, might have made the abstraction of a particle the signal for a riot. And when that acute and excitable race had been crushed under the strong fanaticism of Mohammedan armies, or silenced beneath the dead pressure of Mohammedan fatalism and tyranny; when Church history passed over to the West, and to another range of controversies, the two earlier Creeds had already the sacred halo of antiquity on them; the crystals were set, and no foreign element could blend with them to alter their form.

With the Hymns it might have been otherwise. The strictest research can, it seems, only ascertain their existence in the earliest records, but cannot trace their beginning. That before such a date the "Te Deum" cannot be found, and that in the earliest known Liturgies the "Thrice Holy" can be found, appears nearly all that can be discovered. Whether they sprang first to light in a burst of

[1] Neander's "Church History."

choral song, like that inspired hymn in the Acts; or were bestowed on the Church through the heavenly meditations of one solitary believer; or gradually, like a river, by its tributary streams, rose to what they are, we can perhaps never know.

We all know the tradition, that the "Te Deum" gushed forth in sudden inspiration from the lips of Ambrose, as he baptized Augustine; or (as it exists in another form) that St. Ambrose and St. Augustine, touched at the same moment by the same sacred fire, sang it together in responses. But beautiful as this legend is, and of early origin, those who have searched into the subject more deeply seem to think it must be classed among other beautiful typical stories of the heroic ages of Christendom. There is, however, another theory of the origin of the "Te Deum" (to which Daniel seems to lean) more beautiful and appropriate than even this old legend. It is believed by many to have sprung from an earlier Oriental morning hymn; perhaps to have grown out of fragments of many such hymns. Gradually, therefore, if this be true, it may have flowed on from age to age, gathering fresh tides of truth and melody, till, as you trace back the sacred stream to its source, your exploring feet are checked among the snowy mountains of the distant past; and, listening through the mists and silence, you seem to hear far off the music with which it first wells into light, where the few persecuted Christians of Pliny's days meet before dawn to sing their hymn of praise to Christ as God.

In each of these three Hymns how exulting and

triumphant the strain is! They are hymns of praise of the noblest kind: they are occupied, not with our feelings about the object of adoration, but with the object Himself. Not a tone of sorrow mingles with them; the joy of Redemption altogether overwhelms the lamentation of the Fall; mortality is swallowed up of life.

And yet the first two, at least, were sung before Christianity had achieved any visible triumph; when it was still a *religio illicita*, existing by precarious sufferance, when every public act of Christian worship was liable to end in martyrdom, and every song of praise might be finished among the multitude above, who rejoice that they have been counted worthy to suffer shame for the name of Jesus. Those who joined in it knew not how soon their "Holy, holy, holy," might be resumed, after a brief agony, among "angels and archangels, and all the company of heaven," or whether their "Glory to God in the highest" might not be chanted next among the angelic band who first struck its chords of joy. Was it not that very possibility which gave the peculiar thrill to the words?

"*It is very meet, right, and our bounden duty, that we should at all times, and in all places, give thanks unto Thee, O Lord, Holy Father, Almighty, Everlasting God. Therefore with angels and archangels, and all the company of heaven, we laud and magnify Thy glorious Name; evermore praising Thee, and saying, Holy, holy, holy, Lord God of hosts, heaven and earth are full of Thy glory: Glory be to Thee, O Lord most high.*"

The duty of joy and praise, the sanctity of all places and the fitness of all times for worship! Do we not feel in this glorious burst of thanksgiving the irrepressible joy of redeemed creatures set free from all bondage; sinful yet forgiven, and fighting with God against sin; children, yet children of God coming before their Father with the song He loves to hear; little indeed, and as nothing among the countless hosts of heavenly worshippers, yet still actually amongst them, and no strangers there, because, in God's household, whilst the greatest are as dust before His majesty, the least shine as the sun in His love?

It is as if the veil were for a moment withdrawn, and the whole family in earth and heaven were united in one song. Myriads who sang it once on earth have passed through the veil one by one, and have taken their places in the other choir; and soon the veil must be visibly rent, and the two choirs made one.

The second Hymn after the Communion, like the first, soars away at once from self to God, and rests, not on our joy in God, but on God who is our joy, giving thanks to the Father for His great glory, and to the Son for His redeeming love. Like the "Te Deum," it is chiefly addressed to Christ. But its accents are to accompany us back into the outer world; and the hymn, which began, as it were, among the angels, ends with a Miserere such as befits those yet in the body of death, well as it befitted those many martyrs of early times who, we are told, sang this hymn on their way to martyrdom.

Happy for us if the music of those words sings on in our hearts through the temptations and toils of the following days, and so from hour to hour we make our work keep time to that heavenly melody!

> Glory to God on high,
> And on earth peace,
> Good will towards men.
> We praise Thee,
> We bless Thee,
> We glorify Thee,
> We give thanks to Thee,
> For Thy great glory,
> O Lord God,
> Heavenly King,
> God the Father Almighty.
> O Lord God,
> Only-begotten Son
> Jesu Christ;
> O Lord God,
> Lamb of God,
> Son of the Father
> That takest away the sins of the world,
> Have mercy on us.
> Thou that takest away the sins of the world,
> Have mercy on us.
> Thou that takest away the sins of the world,
> Receive our prayer.
> Thou that sittest at the right hand of God the Father,
> Have mercy on us.
> For Thou only art holy;
> Thou only art the Lord;
> Thou only, O Christ,
> With the Holy Ghost,
> Art most high in the glory of God the Father.

Happy for us when the Gloria and Miserere are ever thus intertwined!

The "Te Deum" completes and crowns this second triad of Christian hymns. It is at once a hymn, a creed, and a prayer; or rather it is a creed taking wing and soaring heavenward; it is faith seized with a sudden joy as she counts her treasures, and laying them at the feet of Jesus in a song; it is the incense of prayer, rising so near the rainbow round the throne as to catch its light and become radiant as well as fragrant, a cloud of incense illumined into a cloud of glory. It is a shrine around which the Church has hung her joys for centuries, and in which each of us has garnered up one sacred memory after another. Year by year its meaning has been unfolded to us. One verse has been a fountain of comfort opened to us in some desert place; others have been unveiled to us in the light of a fresh joy or the darkness of a fresh sorrow; and as our horizon widens, it will expand ever above and beyond, because, and only because, it is full of Him whose fulness filleth all in all.

In the original Latin, subjoined, it has been observed, that, in three places especially, the Latin has a fuller meaning than the English.

The "Martyrum candidatus exercitus" contains an allusion scarcely indicated in the "noble army of martyrs;" an allusion not only to the dazzling festive robes of the Roman noble, but to the "souls under the altar to whom were given white robes, to the white-robed multitude who came out of great tribulation, and had washed their robes and made them white in the blood of the Lamb."

The "Tu ad liberandum suscepturus hominem" expresses not only the truth that our Lord "took on Him to deliver man," but that it was by becoming man He delivered man.

The "Tu devicto mortis aculeo" says, not only "When Thou hadst overcome the sharpness of death," but "When Thou hadst plucked the sting from death."

And as the echoes of the solemn chant die away in village church or cathedral choir, the wish will sometimes arise that the last sound left on the ear could be, not the word "confounded," but as in the Latin, the triumphant "for ever."

Te Deum laudamus : Te Dominum confitemur.
Te æternum Patrem omnis terra veneratur.
Tibi omnes angeli, tibi cœli et universæ potestates,
Tibi cherubim et seraphim, incessabili voce proclamant :
Sanctus, Sanctus, Sanctus, Dominus Deus Sabaoth ;
Pleni sunt cœli et terra majestate gloriæ tuæ.
Te gloriosus apostolorum chorus ;
Te prophetarum laudabilis numerus ;
Te martyrum candidatus laudat exercitus.
Te per orbem terrarum, sancta confitetur ecclesia,
Patrem immensæ majestatis ;
Venerandum tuum verum, et unicum Filium ;
Sanctum quoque Paraclitum Spiritum.
Tu Rex gloriæ, Christe :
Tu Patris sempiternus es Filius.
Tu ad liberandum suscepturus hominem, non horruisti
    virginis uterum ;
Tu, devicto mortis aculeo, aperuisti credentibus regna
    cœlorum.
Tu ad dexteram Dei sedes in gloria Patris.

Judex crederis esse venturus :
Te, ergo quæsumus, famulis tuis subveni, quos pretioso sanguine redemisti.
Æterna fac cum sanctis tuis in gloria numerari.
Salvum fac populum tuum, Domine : et benedic hæreditati tuæ.
Et rege eos, et extolle illos usque in æternum.
Per singulos dies benedicimus te.
Et laudamus nomen tuum in sæculum : et in sæculum sæculi.
Dignare, Domine, die isto sine peccato nos custodire.
Miserere nostri Domine : miserere nostri.
Fiat misericordia tua, Domine, super nos, quemadmodum speravimus in te.
In te Domine speravi : non confundar in æternum.

CHAPTER III

THE ANONYMOUS GREEK HYMNS

IT may be well to dwell on the anonymous early hymns before we enter on the compositions of any known author; because where the author is not ascertained (and the date thus fixed), whilst the style is simple and primitive, the earliest manuscript discovered may be but a copy of earlier writings, and a record of some far earlier unwritten song. For instance, the "Gloria in Excelsis," sometimes called a Morning Hymn or the "Hymnus Angelicus," preserved in our Communion Service, is possibly or probably more ancient than anything Clement of Alexandria, the earliest known hymn-writer, ever wrote. Its sublime simplicity would lead one to conclude it must be so, were Christianity merely an historical religion. As it is, the question of comparative chronology seems of little importance. The original authentic documents of our faith are in our hands, and these we all acknowledge as our standard of doctrine; and the Fountain of our life is equally near to every age. Whether, therefore, the greater purity of many of these anonymous hymns arises from their greater antiquity, or from a fresh approach to that ever-present Fountain in an age when many had recourse to polluted waters and broken cisterns, is a problem we may contentedly leave unsolved. In either case, they bear witness to a living communion of some human hearts with God, and are as such most precious, whether we regard them as carrying up the links of our faith to the first century, or as bringing down the faith and worship of the apostolic age to the fourth century.

The first of these anonymous hymns which may be given here are those called in Daniel's "Thesaurus," Morning and Evening Hymn; the Morning Hymn being the well-known "Glory to God in the highest."

MORNING HYMN.

Daniel, vol. iii. p. 4, "Thesaurus Hymnologicus."

Glory to God in the highest,
And on earth peace,
Good will towards men.
We praise Thee,
We bless Thee,
We glorify Thee,
We give thanks to Thee,
For Thy great glory,
O Lord, heavenly King,
God the Father Almighty.
O Lord, the only-begotten Son,
Jesu Christ,

And the Holy Ghost.[1]
O Lord God,
Lamb of God,
Son of the Father,
Thou that takest away the sins of the world,
Receive our prayer.
Thou that sittest at the right hand of the Father,
Have mercy on us.
For Thou only art holy,
Thou only art the Lord,
O Jesu Christ,
To the glory of God the Father. Amen.

EVENING HYMN.

Daniel, vol. iii. p. 5.

Joyful light of holy glory,
Of the immortal Heavenly Father,
Holy, blessed
Jesu Christ,
We, coming at the setting of the sun,
Beholding the evening light,
Praise Father and Son
And Holy Spirit, God.
Thee it is meet
At all hours to praise
With sacred voices, Son of God,
Thou who givest life;
Therefore the world glorifies Thee.

In this last hymn there is no fancy, no ecstasy of emotion. The poetry consists in the faith, in the

---

[1] It will be observed that there are a few slight variations between this version of the hymn, which is taken from the Greek, in Daniel's "Thesaurus," and that in the Prayer-book.

vision of the Invisible. The praise is not so much the utterance of man's feelings as of God's name. The images are so simple as to be scarcely images at all, but only the clearest expression of truth. And yet what sweeter or sublimer evening thoughts could any desire to rest the heart upon!

The sun is setting; the brief twilight of Egypt, Syria, or Greece, making scarcely any interval between day and night, is beginning. The glow of the golden southern day is gone; in another minute the glorious southern sun has sunk suddenly in his majesty and strength, as he arose; and night, with its silence and cold dews, is coming. The little band of persecuted Christians, whom no danger could deprive of the joy of meeting to claim their Lord's promise to the "two or three," have gathered by the river side, in the upper chamber, or in the inner court; or, in later times, amidst the great spaces of the Oriental cathedral at Antioch, Constantinople, or Alexandria, among the heavy shadows of buildings meant rather to exclude than to admit the dazzling southern sunshine, the great Christian assembly has met. The visible sun has gone, but the Church is a dweller in perpetual light. Christians are children of the day, and they have met to gaze in faith on Him whose presence makes day and heaven, Christ the light of holy glory, the giver of life.

The next Evening Hymn is probably of a much later date, and of a different character. It is the aspiration of a single heart, once oppressed with sins and conscious of danger; but it has its own interest, as in its simple accents we listen to the secret supplications of one who fought the good fight more than a thousand years ago.

EVENING HYMN.

Daniel, vol. iii. p. 127.

The day is passing on,
I thank Thee, O Lord.
I beseech Thee this evening and this night
Keep me without sin,
Saviour, and save me!

The day is passing away,
I glorify Thee, O Master.
I beseech Thee this evening and this night
Keep me without offence,
Saviour, and save me!

The day has pass'd away,
I praise Thee, Holy One.
I beseech Thee this evening and this night
Keep me free from snares,
Saviour, and save me!

Enlighten mine eyes,
Christ, O God,
That I sleep not unto death;
Let not mine enemy say,
I have prevail'd against him!

Be the guard of my soul,
O God, for I pass on
Through the midst of snares;
Deliver me from them and save,
Thou Gracious One, who lovest men!

Before passing on from the hymns which refer to special seasons of the day, one more may be given, which seems intended for waking hours at night. It seems a response to the Psalmist's "At midnight will I arise, and sing praises unto Thee," and solemnly must the words have echoed through the silence.

AN ECHO.

Daniel, vol. iii. p. 126.

Being raised up from sleep
We fall before Thee, gracious One,
And we cry aloud the angels' hymn
To Thee, mighty One.
Holy, holy, art Thou, O God;
For Thy mercy's sake have mercy on us.

From the couch and from sleep
Thou raisest me, O Lord!
Enlighten my mind and my heart,
And open Thou my lips,
That I may praise Thee, holy Trinity:
Holy, holy, holy, art Thou.

The Judge will come with a great multitude,
And the deeds of each one shall be laid bare;
But with fear we will cry in the midst of the night,
Holy, holy, holy, art Thou.

By far the greater number of the anonymous hymns are inspired, not by special circumstances in the writer's life, but by the contemplation of Christ —His birth, baptism, death, resurrection, and ascension. Of these the larger proportion are suggested by His nativity, involving the incarnation, the union of the Godhead and humanity in His person, and the glad tidings of great joy.

ON THE NATIVITY OF CHRIST.

Daniel, vol. iii. p. 126.

Make ready, O Bethlehem!
Eden is open'd to all;
Prepare, O Ephratah!
For the Tree of Life
Has come forth in the cave
From the Virgin. Paradise
Thus did her womb become,
In which was the Divine Tree,
Of which we eat and live.
Not like Adam shall we die,
For Christ is born
To raise again the fallen image,
And transform it by partaking it.

AGAIN ON THE NATIVITY.

Daniel, vol. iii. p. 129.

Thy birth, O Christ our God,
Has caused to rise on the world the light of knowledge;
For by it, the worshippers of the stars
Were taught by a star to worship Thee,
The Sun of righteousness, and to know Thee,
The Dayspring from on high. O Lord, glory to Thee!
The first-fruits of the Gentiles, Heaven
Gather'd in to Thee, a babe lying in the manger.
Calling the wise men by a star,
Astonish'd to behold,
Not sceptre and throne, but the uttermost poverty;
For what poorer than a cave?
And what meaner than swaddling clothes?
Through which shone the riches of Thy Deity.
O Lord, glory to Thee!

NATAL HYMN.

Daniel, vol. iii. p. 130.

The Virgin to-day
Bears the Infinite,
And the earth draws near
In the cave to the Inaccessible.
Angels with shepherds
Render homage;
Magi with stars
Shew the way;
Since for our sakes
The God from eternity has become the new-born babe.

DOXOLOGY.

Daniel, vol. iii. p. 131.

Thy pure image we worship,
O good Lord, beseeching Thee,
Pardon our failures.
Christ, our God!
Thou wast content in Thy good will
To come in the flesh,
That Thou mightest redeem those Thou hadst made
From the bondage of the enemy.
Wherefore, thankfully we cry unto Thee,
Who fillest all with joy!
Our Saviour, who didst appear
To save the world!

HYMN.

Daniel, vol. iii. p. 131.

The Mystery hidden from the ages,
And unknown to angels,

Through a virgin made manifest to those on the earth,
God uniting Himself to flesh
Without confounding the substance,
And voluntarily enduring the cross for us;
By which, restoring the first Adam,
He saved our souls from death.

ON THE BAPTISM OF CHRIST.

Daniel, vol. iii. p. 132.

Christ, compassionate to all,
Taking away the multitude of transgressions
By immeasurable mercy;
Thou comest as man
To be baptized in the waters of Jordan,
Clothing me with the robe of glory,
Before miserably stripped of all.

ON THE SAME.

Daniel, vol. iii. p. 132.

When Thou wast baptized in Jordan, O Christ,
The worship of the Trinity was revealed;
For the voice of the Father bears witness to Thee,
Calling Thee the beloved Son;
And the Spirit, in the form of a dove,
Confirmed the sure word.
O Christ, God made manifest,
And illuminating the world, glory to Thee!

ON THE EPIPHANY.

Daniel, vol. iii. p. 133.

When in Thy Epiphany, Thou didst enlighten all things,
Then the salt sea of unbelief fled,

And down-flowing Jordan turned its course,
Lifting us upwards to heaven.
But in the height of Thy Divine commandments
Keep us, Christ, O God, and save us.

The five following hymns are, however, on the Crucifixion and the Resurrection. They are enough to show what the faith of those who sang them was; and the triumphal tone of the grand chant of victory rings through them all:—

TO CHRIST ON THE CROSS.

Daniel, vol. iii. p. 134.

Thou who, on the sixth day and hour,
Didst nail to the cross the sin
Which Adam dared in paradise;
Rend also the handwriting of our transgressions,
O Christ, our God, and save us!

TO THE SAME.

Daniel, vol. iii. p. 134.

Thou workest salvation in the midst of the earth,
Christ, O God, stretching on the cross Thy spotless hands;
Gathering in all the nations as they cry,
O Lord, glory to Thee!

ON THE RESURRECTION.

Daniel, vol. iii. p. 135.

To-day, salvation to the world!
We gather together to Him who has risen from the tomb;
The Prince of life, Christ our God;
Taking away death,
He gave the victory to us,
And the great mercy.

Christ is risen from the dead!
In death trampling on death;
And on those in the graves
Bestowing life.

Beholding the resurrection of Christ,
We worship the holy Lord,
Jesus, the only sinless One.
Thy cross, O Christ, we adore,
And Thy holy resurrection
We praise and glorify.

By Thy body in the grave,
By Thy soul in Hades,
As God in paradise with the thief,
And on the throne, art Thou by Thine essence, O Christ,
With the Father and the Spirit,
Filling all things—the Incomprehensible.

Life-giving, more pleasant than paradise,
More glorious than any bridal-chamber of kings,
Appears Thy sepulchre, O Christ,
The fountain of our resurrection.
Taking our form on Thee,
And enduring the cross bodily,
Save me by Thy resurrection,
Christ, O God, who lovest men!

From the highest, full of pity, Thou camest down,
Wast laid for three days in the grave,
That Thou mightest free us from suffering:
Our life, and our resurrection,
O Lord, glory to Thee!

ON THE ASCENSION.

Daniel, vol. iii. p. 136.

Thou art received up into glory, O Christ our God,
Having made glad Thy disciples
By the promise of the Holy Spirit,
Strengthening them by Thy blessing:
For Thou art the Son of God,
The Redeemer of the world.

When Thou hadst fulfill'd the dispensation for us,
And united things on earth to heaven,
Thou wast received up into glory, O Christ our God.
Yet, even there not parted from us, but abiding
Unsever'd from those who love Thee.
"I am with you, and none against you."

ON PENTECOST.

Daniel, vol. iii. p. 136.

When, descending, He confused the tongues,
The Highest scatter'd the nations;
When He distributed the tongues of fire,
He call'd all to unity:
Thus, with one voice, we glorify the All-holy Spirit.

The following is more subjective than any of the others, and reminds us more of the Moravian hymns, or of some of those of the Middle Ages:—

SWEET THOUGHTS, WITH REPENTANCE TO JESUS.

Daniel, vol. iii. p. 127.

Most sweet Jesus, long-suffering Jesus,
Heal the wounds of my soul,

Jesus, and sweeten my heart.
I pray Thee, most merciful Jesus, my Saviour,
That I, saved, may magnify Thee.

Hear me, my Saviour, lover of man,
Thy servant crying in affliction,
And deliver me, Jesus, from judgment
And from punishment, only One, long-suffering,
Most sweet Jesus, only One, most merciful.

Receive Thy servant, my Saviour,
Falling before Thee with tears, my Saviour;
And save, Jesus, me repenting,
And from hell, O Master, redeem me, Jesus;
Heal, my Saviour, my soul
Of its wounds, Jesus, I pray Thee:

And with Thine hand rescue me, my Saviour;
Compassionate, from the soul-murderer Satan; and save me.
I have sinned, my most sweet Saviour;
Merciful, my Saviour, save me,
Fleeing to Thy defence, long-suffering Jesus,
And make me meet for Thy kingdom.

Thou, O Jesus, art the light of my mind,
Thou art the salvation of my lost soul;—
Thou the Saviour, O Jesus, from punishment
And from hell deliver me, weeping like a helpless child.
Save, O Jesus; O my Christ, save me, miserable.

Surely in these words we can feel the tears with which they must have been broken, when first uttered by lips so long since silent in the grave. And surely the sobbing prayer was heard, and all through these ages the answer has been pouring forth in praise in heaven.

These early hymns have indeed this characteristic: they are "sung unto the Lord." They are full of faith in a personal, listening Saviour. The name of Jesus is in them no mere summary of a system of doctrines, but the name of a living, gracious, mighty, and beloved Friend. Some of them are so true and so tender, so sublime in their simplicity, so full of the repose of faith, and so free from the flutter of fancy, so soaring above self to God in lowly, happy adoration, that one would delight to think they may have been among the psalms, and hymns, and spiritual songs to which St. Paul listened, or the "beloved disciple," when in his old age he would be led to meet the Church, silently to join their worship, and say at parting, "Little children, love one another."

But we know not. The name of the "master" has perished, and the strain floats down to us, unlimited by any personal associations, a part of the one great song. As in a beautiful cathedral, of which the architect's name is lost, we cannot say, "This is that man's work;" but we may say instead, "This is God's house; let us worship Him." Surely could the singers stoop from their places among the blessed and listen, they would ask no more.

We may close this chapter with an anonymous Oriental doxology, with which we might well be content at last to close our psalm of life:—

Daniel, vol. iii. p. 138.

God is my hope,
Christ is my refuge,
The Holy Spirit is my vesture;
Holy Trinity, glory to Thee.

CHAPTER IV

CLEMENT OF ALEXANDRIA, EPHREM SYRUS, AND GREGORY OF NAZIANZUM

WE come now to another level, more within the ordinary horizon of sacred song; to hymns whose range has been less extended, and of whose writers we can form a more definite picture. The singers as well as the songs become perceptible; although in some instances the songs seem more familiar to us, less estranged by the foreign garb of distant lands and ages than the singers. The truths of the hymns come home to our hearts, whilst the mode of life and thought of the writers often seems difficult to understand.

Of all the cities on that great inland sea which once washed the shores of every civilized state in the world, perhaps none serve better as a tide-mark to show how far the centre of the social world has glided westward than Alexandria. Rome is still imperial, and it is the nature rather than the locality of her empire which has changed; Constantinople is still the centre of its own system, feeble and ruinous as both centre and system are; Jerusalem, as of old, is the holy city of faith; but Alexandria, still indeed busy and flourishing, is busy and flourishing only as the channel of traffic from western regions, which were back-woods and copper-diggings when her palaces first rose. White palaces and quays still gleam across the blue Mediterranean, breaking the sandy glow of the flat Egyptian shores; the streets are thronged with eager motley crowds; and luxurious villas, with their gardens, fringe the suburbs. But the motion is galvanic, communicated by impulse from without, not flowing from life within: English and French merchants are her princes; the city is but a great inn on the overland route; and if the great Oriental traffic could find other channels, Alexandria might soon sink into a silent, ruinous, dreamy Turkish village, like Tyre or Sidon. Sixteen hundred years ago it was indeed different; and to understand in any measure any life which was lived there then, we must clothe the skeleton,— we must transform the dry, dead names in the ancient atlas into pictures.

About the close of the second century, when Clement was called to be the head of the catechetical school at Alexandria, he was called to a centre of thought and life from which the slightest touch vibrated in a thousand directions. His own intellectual history illustrates strongly the contrast between the past and the present. He seems to have been a merchantman seeking goodly pearls, until he found at length the pearl of great price. He wandered restlessly from school to school, seeking, it seems, not to become learned, but to find truth: not content, as an intellectual curiosity hunter, to hoard up treasures of information, he wanted some living truth to live upon. His search was long. One of his teachers came from Ionia, the old birthplace of Greek science and poetry,—fires not yet quite burned into ashes. Clement seems, however, chiefly to have drawn from Oriental sources. His two next teachers were a Cœlo-Syrian and an Assyrian; names that recall associations too ancient and shadowy to picture,—histories whose skeleton is scarcely left to us, but only the dry embalmed mummy, which passes into dust as you open the tomb, before you can tell what you have seen. Did thoughtful and educated men, indeed, then live on the Cœlo-Syrian plain, and converse beneath the grand porticoes of the temples at Baalbec? Were animated philosophical debates held under the shadow of those magnificent columns which now stand so solitary and obsolete, scarcely able to tell us their own story? And at night, when the glorious Syrian moon silvered the snows of Lebanon, and threw the gigantic shadows of those temples across the great spaces of their courts, did men watch there whom all this beauty led to question what lay beneath and beyond? Many centuries have passed, indeed, since men have looked for intellectual light, as Clement did, from Asia Minor, Assyria, or the Lebanon plains. The heavy black pall of Mohammedanism, the crushing weight of Turkish rule, has fallen over them all.

Clement had one other teacher, a Jew from Palestine. The great light which shone for a time in bodily presence on the shores of the Sea of Galilee had been rejected, and had withdrawn itself. The sentence of death had fallen on the cities of Galilee; but it was not yet executed to the full. Tiberias was the seat of a school of Jewish rabbis; and on the shores of the Sea of Galilee, Clement could still listen to the voices of scribes and Pharisees, himself yet ignorant of the voice which had silenced their lifeless commentaries; of the beneficent footsteps which had once trodden those shores and those waves, bringing health to the sick and suffering there.

But it was at Alexandria that Clement first learned the Divine Word which could solve the riddles of philosophers and rabbis. Here at length he found what he had unconsciously sought: redemption and spiritual strength in a living Redeemer. And here his wanderings ended. Pantænus, the catechetical Christian teacher from whom he learnt Christianity after a time went as a missionary into India, and Clement took his place. He had found a truth it was worth while to spend life in communicating. For such a mission no more central spot existed than Alexandria; a mart, as now, of Eastern and Western traffic, merchants resorted thither from all quarters. To the south stretched the great Egyptian granary of Rome; along the coasts of Syria, and Asia Minor, and Northern Africa, were rich cultivated lands and a busy manufacturing population; the seas all around were specked with countless sails of vessels, trading in short voyages from island to island and city to city. With their merchandise, these vessels, like the Alexandrian corn-ship once wrecked at Melita, carried the heralds of the new doctrine of the Kingdom of God. The commercial cities where the Jews had planted their synagogues became everywhere the sites of infant churches. At Alexandria was the great mint and exchange for Oriental and European thought. Mystical and undefined Oriental visions, acute and comprehensive Greek theories, narrow and imperious rabbinical dogmas met here, and were exchanged or re-coined.

In the midst of all these Clement taught; not so much in the pulpit of a lecture-room or a church, as in the philosopher's cloak, pacing up and down the shady porticoes. To him these varied phases of thought were no mere theories known as to a critic from outside: he had learned them by trying them. Many of these streams had flowed in succession through his own mind, and he knew what they could give, and what they could not give. They had formed part, not merely of the catalogue of his acquirements, but of the experience of his heart. In these respects he had some of the qualifications of St. Paul. But the flood of Christian truth had not rushed with such force through his mind as entirely to sweep away all remains of falsehood, leaving, as with St. Paul, only the sympathy of memory with those in error. His eyes do not seem always to have been clear to see the grandeur of simple truth above the high-sounding theories of his time. He did not, it would seem, always perceive how much deeper the simplest faith which brings into communion with God is, than the most profound reasoning about the things of God. The fashion of this world, and therefore the doom of this world, seem to have been on some of his teaching, and so far it has "passed away;" yet many words are quoted from his writings, immortal because really living. Although we know absolutely nothing of Clement except of his intellectual or spiritual history; although his home, if he had one, is altogether hidden from us, and he is to us rather a voice than a man; yet we must indeed draw near to the heart from which flowed such words as these:

"Prayer, if I may speak so boldly, is intercourse with God. Even if we do but lisp, even though we silently address God without opening our lips, yet we cry to Him in the inmost recesses of the heart; for God always listens to the sincere direction of the heart to Him."

And again, we feel how closely knowledge and faith must have been interwoven in him when he says of a true Christian,—

"He will pray in every place, but not openly, to be seen of men. Even when he is walking for recreation, in his converse with others, in silence, in reading, in all rational pursuits, he finds opportunity for prayer; and although he is only thinking on God in the little chamber of his soul, and calling on his Father with silent aspiration, God is near him and with him, for he is still speaking to Him."

To Clement "not the place was the church, but the congregation of the elect;" and he recommended the Christian husband and wife to consecrate each day by commencing it with reading the Bible and prayer.

Such was the earliest Christian hymn-writer whose name has come down to us. The one hymn which is attributed to him is, indeed, rather a catalogue of scriptural figures than an outburst of glowing adoration; but it gives a deep meaning to every word of it to link it with Clement's own description of the perils amidst which it was written. "Daily," he wrote, "martyrs are burned, beheaded, and crucified before our eyes." He himself was at length obliged to flee for his life from Alexandria; and of his subsequent history scarcely anything is known. The catalogue of images in the hymn, of which the following lines are an attempt at a translation, must surely have been to Clement a catalogue of treasures which he found in Christ, and in which he rejoiced :—

HYMN OF THE SAVIOUR CHRIST.

Daniel, vol. iii. p. 3. 1.

Mouth of babes who cannot speak,
Wing of nestlings who cannot fly,
Sure Guide of babes,
Shepherd of royal sheep,
Gather Thine own
Artless children,
To praise in holiness,
To sing in guilelessness,
With blameless lips,
Thee, O Christ, Guide of children.

Christ, King of Saints,
All-governing Word
Of the Highest Father,
Chief of wisdom,

Support of toil,
Ever-rejoicing,
Of mortal race,
Saviour Jesus,
Shepherd, Husbandman,
Helm, Rein !

Heavenly wing
Of Thy all-white flock ;
Fisher of men,
Of the saved,
From the sea of evil—
The helpless fish
From the hostile wave
By sweet life enticing.

Lead, O Shepherd
Of reasoning sheep ;
Holy One, lead—
King of speechless children !

The footsteps of Christ
Are the heavenly way.
Ever-flowing Word,
Infinite Age,
Perpetual Light,
Fountain of mercy,
Worker of virtue,
Holy sustenance
Of those who praise God,—Christ Jesus !
The heavenly milk
Of the sweet breasts
Of the bride of graces,
Pressed out of Thy wisdom.

These babes
With tender lips
Nourished ;
By the dew of the Spirit
Replenished ;
Their artless praises,
Their true hymns,
O Christ our King,
Sacred rewards (products)
Of the doctrine of life,
We hymn together,
We hymn in simplicity,
The Mighty Child.
The chorus of peace,
The kindred of Christ,
The race of the temperate,
We will praise together the God of peace.

Through all the images here so quaintly interwoven—like a stained window, of which the eye loses the design in the complication of colours—we may surely trace, as in quaint old letters on a scroll winding through all the mosaic of tints, " Christ all in all." And could the earliest Christian hymn bear a nobler inscription ? Yet, at the same time, we must remember that whilst the truth of the early Christian writings bears precious testimony to the Christian life of the times, their defects and mistakes bear by contrast no less valuable testimony to the fuller inspiration of those earlier writings in which such defects and exaggerations are not found.

More than a century passes between the days of Clement and the next hymn-writer whose name is known; and of him we know little but the name.

Ephrem Syrus was a monk and a deacon, and lived in that "land beyond the flood" from which Abraham was called to be a pilgrim and a stranger in the land of promise. Monasticism was becoming more and more the one accepted type of a religious life, and Ephrem is spoken of as a man of learning and a monk. Yet his hymns breathe much of the fragrance of a home. They seem remarkable for childlike simplicity and much tenderness of natural feeling. There is a simple joyousness about his thanksgivings. He seems to have loved to dwell on such themes as the infancy of the Saviour, the hosannas of the children, the happiness of those who died in childhood. One can fancy little children clustering round his knee, and learning from his lips to lisp such words as these :—

THE CHILDREN IN PARADISE.

Daniel, vol. iii. p. 155. VI.

To Thee, O God, be praises
From lips of babes and sucklings,
As in the heavenly meadows
    Like spotless lambs they feed,

'Mid leafy trees they pasture—
Thus saith the blessed Spirit;
And Gabriel, prince of angels,
    That happy flock doth lead.

The messengers of Heaven,
With sons of light united,
In purest regions dwelling,
    No curse or woe they see.

And at the Resurrection
With joy arise their bodies;
Their spirits knew no bondage,
    Their bodies now are free.

Brief here below their sojourn;
Their dwelling is in Eden,
And one bright day their parents
    Hope yet with them to be.

Christian children of those distant times might thus, as they thought of their little brothers and sisters in the grave, sing, " We are seven."

They could also learn to echo the chant of the children who cried Hosanna before Him who had taken the little ones in His arms and blessed them, as (perhaps in the very language of the children of Jerusalem) they sang these words of Ephrem :—

ON PALM SUNDAY.

Daniel, vol. iii, p. 163. ix.

Salem is shouting with her children,
    Praise Him who comes, and is to come;
Hosanna, here and in the highest,
    Be to the Father's mighty Son.

Praise Him who once Himself did humble,
    In love, to save our human race;
Praise Him who all the world doth gladden
    With God his Father's boundless grace.

O Lord, who would not gaze and wonder
    To see how low has stooped Thy love!
The cherubim on fiery chariots
    Thy glory humbly bear above.

And here an ass's foal doth bear Thee,
  Thee in Thy might and holiness;
Because Thou camest, in Thy pity,
  Our fallen race to save and bless.

This day of joy to all creation,
  My happy soul shall have her psalm;
And bear her branches of thanksgiving,
  As those bore branches once of palm.

Before the foal the children strewed them,
  Owning Thy hidden majesty;
Hosanna to the Son of David,
  We with the children cry to Thee.

ON THE TRIUMPHAL ENTRY OF JESUS INTO JERUSALEM.
Daniel, vol. iii. p. 160. VIII.

He calls us to a day of gladness,
  Who came to us the King's own Son;
Go forth with boughs of palm to meet Him,
  And Him with loud hosannas own.

The angels are with us rejoicing,
  Angelic trumpets swell our song;
All nations in one joy uniting,
  Hosanna sounds in every tongue.

To thee, O Lord, loud praise ascendeth,
  From every creature in its kind;
Thee, with an awed and quiv'ring motion,
  Exalteth every waving wind.

The heavens in their quiet beauty
  Praise Thy essential majesty;
The heights rejoice from which Thou camest,
  The depths spring up to welcome Thee.

The sea exults to feel Thy footsteps,
    The land Thy tread, Lord, knoweth well;
Our human nature brings thanksgivings,
    Because Thy Godhead there doth dwell.

To-day the sun rejoicing shineth,
    With happy radiance tenfold bright,
In homage to that Sun of glory
    Which brings to all the nations light.

The moon shall shed her fairest lustre
    O'er all the heavens her softest glow,
Thee on her radiant heights adoring,
    Who for our sakes hast stooped so low.

And all the starry hosts of heaven,
    In festive robes of light array'd,
Shall bring their festal hymns as offerings
    To Him who all so fair hath made.

To-day the forests are rejoicing,
    Each tree its own sweet anthem sings,
Because we wave their leafy branches
    As banners for the King of kings.

To-day let all the brute creation,
    Rejoicing, be no longer dumb;
For lowly on the foal He sitteth,—
    The Heavenly One to us hath come.

Let every village, every city,
    In happy tumult sing His name,
Since even infant lips are shouting,
    "Blessed is He, the King who came!"

Throughout those of his hymns translated into German in Daniel's "Thesaurus," there is a Christian feeling far deeper than the Manicheism (so often reproduced in such varied forms) which looked on visible nature and natural emotion as at war with God. In a hymn on the Nativity, he imagines all creation thronging round the infant Saviour; the shepherds bringing Him offerings from their flocks—"a lamb to the Paschal Lamb, to the First-born a first-born;" the lamb bleating its praises to Him whose coming freed lambs and oxen from sacrifice, since He Himself, the "Lamb of God," has brought us the true perpetual Easter festival. The shepherds praise Him, "the chief Shepherd, who shall gather all in one flock, the Child older than Noah, and younger:"—

Daniel, vol. iii. p. 148.

> Thy father David once
> To save a lamb a lion slew; but Thou,
> O David's Son, destroyest that fierce wolf,
> Invisible, who slew of old Adam,
> A spotless lamb, pastured in paradise.

Old men, and grey-haired women, crowd out of the city of David to greet Him; young men, maidens and mothers, gather around Him who came to consecrate every aspect of human life.

It is a touching allegory, rising far indeed above the narrow horizon of monasticism.

The following lines on the Epiphany must be given in full. They may be called

THE STAR OF BETHLEHEM.

Daniel, vol. iii. p. 150.

> A star shines forth in heaven suddenly,
> A wondrous orb, less than the sun—yet greater;—

Less in its outward light, in inward glory
Greater, pointing to a mystery.
That morning-star sent forth its beams afar
Into the land of those who had no light,
Led them as blind men, by a way they knew not,
Until they came and saw the Light of men,
Offer'd their gifts, received eternal life,
Worshipp'd—and went their way.
Thus had the Son two heralds, one on high
And one below. Above—the star rejoiced;
Below—the Baptist bore him record:
Two heralds thus, one heavenly, one of earth;
That witnessing the nature of the Son,
The majesty of God, and this His human nature.
O mighty wonder! thus were they the heralds
Both of His Godhead and His manhood.
Who held Him only for a son of earth,
To such the star proclaim'd His heavenly glory;
Who held him only for a heavenly spirit,
To such the Baptist spoke of Him as man.
And the holy temple Simeon held the babe
Fast in his aged arms, and sang to Him—

> To me, in Thy mercy,
>   An old man, Thou art come;
> Thou layest my body
>   In peace in the tomb.
> Thou soon wilt awake me,
>   And bid me arise;
> Wilt lead me transfigured
>   To paradise.

Then Anna took the babe upon her arms,
And press'd her mouth upon His infant lips;
Then came the Holy Spirit on her lips,

As erst upon Isaiah's, when the coal
Had touch'd his silent lips, and open'd them:
With glowing heart she sang—

> O Son of the King!
>   Though Thy birth-place was mean,
> All-hearing, yet silent,
>   All-seeing, unseen,
> Unknown, yet all-knowing,
>   God, and yet Son of man!
>   Praise to Thy name.

The hymn next translated seems very true and beautiful in its contrast of faith and natural feeling. It was to be sung at the funerals of children, probably chiefly of choristers; and is called

LAMENT OF A FATHER ON THE DEATH OF HIS LITTLE SON.[1]

FOR THE FUNERALS OF BOYS.

Daniel, vol. iii. p. 151.

> Child, by God's sweet mercy given
>   Through a mortal birth to be;
> Entering this world of sorrows,
>   By His grace, so fair to see;
> Fair as some sweet flower in summer,
>   Till death's hand on thee was laid,
> Scorch'd the beauty from my flower,
>   Made the tender petals fade.

---

[1] The hymns of Ephrem Syrus given here are not, like all the rest in this volume, fresh translations from the original, but translations from the German translation in Daniel. This title, "Lament of a Father," is Daniel's. This hymn may, as Daniel's title suggests, have been written in sympathy with bereaved parents, or, as has been supposed by another translator, in lamentation for one of St. Ephrem's choristers.

Yet I dare not weep nor murmur,
  For I know the King of kings
Leads thee to his marriage-chamber,
  To the glorious bridal brings.

Nature fain would have me weeping,
  Love asserts her mournful right;
But I answer, they have brought thee
  To the happy world of light.
And I fear that my lamentings,
  As I speak thy cherish'd name,
Desecrate the Royal dwelling;—
  Fear to meet deservèd blame,
If I press with tears of anguish
  Into the abode of joy;
Therefore will I, meekly bowing,
  Offer thee to God, my boy.

Yet thy voice, thy childish singing,
  Soundeth ever in my ears;
And I listen, and remember,
  Till mine eyes will gather tears,
Thinking of thy pretty prattlings,
  And thy childish words of love;
But when I begin to murmur,
  Then my spirit looks above,
Listens to the songs of spirits—
  Listens, longing, wondering,
To the ceaseless glad Hosannas
  Angels at thy bridal sing.

There is also a song of Ephrem's about Paradise, the feet of whose mountains the highest waves of the Deluge could but touch and kiss, and reverently turn aside; where the sons of light tread the sea like Peter, and sail the ether on their chariots of cloud. And there is a hymn on the Resurrection, full of beautiful images, or rather visions; the gates of paradise opening of themselves to the just; the guardian angel striking his harp as he goes forth to meet them, when "the Bridegroom comes with songs of joy from the East, and the kingdom of Death is made desolate, as the children of Adam rise from the dust, and soar to meet their Lord." There is mention also of a fire to be passed through ere paradise is reached (a fire at once purgatorial and testing), the unjust being devoured by it, and the just gliding through unharmed. His own anticipations of life after death seem to have been of a pure paradise, and a joyful dwelling with Christ. He has in one poem a fine image of Satan and Death listening astounded to the song of the angels at the birth of Jesus: Satan flies into the wilderness, and Death into the abyss.

> Then, because they fled from Him,
> Jesus track'd them to their lairs :
> Went into the wilderness,
> Vanquishing the devil there.
> To the depths of death descending,
> There o'ercame the might of death.
> Thus were both the foes led captive
> Who had robb'd our race of hope.
> Therefore blooms sweet hope on earth :
> In the highest, joy, as thence
> Came the angels to mankind
> With the tidings of great joy.

Such are some specimens of the sacred singing of Ephrem, monk of Mesopotamia. His learning might seem foolishness to children among us, as our science may to those who follow us; and his theology may have fallen short of the fulness and simplicity of the apostles' teaching; but his heart seems to have been steeped in the Gospel histories; and in those Gospels he surely found the Saviour, whom not having seen he loved, and in whom he rejoiced with joy unspeakable and full of glory, receiving the end of his faith, even the salvation of his soul.

One other golden saying comes from the heart of the old singer to ours; it is in one of his exhortations in the Church services, and might make a motto for many an hour of united or secret prayer: "*In the very moment when thou prayest, a treasure is laid up for thee in heaven.*" No Christian prayer falls back from the closed gates of heaven; each enters there like a messenger-dove; some bring back immediate visible answers, but all enrich our store of blessings there, and all return to the heart with the fragrance of peace on them from the holy place where they have been. And if Ephrem the Syrian writes this joyful truth deeper on our hearts, it surely must be because God wrote it on his own.

The life of Gregory of Nazianzum is less hidden from us than that of Ephrem Syrus. He appears to us not as a mere solitary, but as a son, a brother, and a friend. The name of his mother, Nonna, is among the happy list of those who have been invested with woman's sweetest dignity, the training of a son for God. Nonna, the mother of Gregory, is among the blessed band which includes Anthusa, the early widowed mother of Chrysostom; and

Monica, the mother of Augustine, patient in hope through her son's many wanderings. On Nonna another great honour also was bestowed. The consistency of her piety, and the influence of her gentle, loving, Christian character, led her husband from a half-pagan sect to the truth; after which he became bishop of Nazianzum in Cappadocia. Gregory, like Samuel, was the child of many prayers. He himself compares his mother to Hannah. Soon after his birth he was taken to the altar, and there solemnly dedicated to God, a volume of the Gospels being laid on his infant hands, in token of the service to which he was destined. All through his childhood and youth the light of his mother's piety continued to shine on him. We hear little of the words she said, but those around her felt that her faith was a constant well-spring of joy. Her delight in meditating on the facts of our redemption,—on the birth, and death, and resurrection of the Lord,—was so great, that on a festival-day, whatever her anxieties or bodily sufferings, she was never known to be sad; and at last she died in prayer before the altar. Doubtless her influence was a spell which made a sacred calm around Gregory in many a storm of the tumultuous days he lived in. As he grew up he pursued his studies at Alexandria, and afterwards at Athens, where he formed a close friendship with Basil, a student from his own province of Cappadocia. They pursued the same studies, and, in looking forward to life, their dreams and projects placed them always side by side. The profession for which they had both been originally destined was rhetoric, and Athens at that time was still a stronghold of Paganism. The worship of the old gods lingered around their ancient temples, and the Emperor Julian was a fellow-student with Gregory and Basil. But on both the friends had rested the strong influence of early religious training. Basil came of an ancient Christian family, and counted among his ancestry sufferers for the faith. As in the case of Timothy, the faith which dwelt in him had first dwelt in his mother and his grandmother, Emmelia and Macrina. A pious elder sister had continued the same holy influence after the death of their mother. The piety of Gregory and Basil, ascetic as it became, seems never to have altogether lost the softening effect of those healthy home influences. There is a playfulness and life about some of their letters, which breathe more of the home than of the monastery. Together they formed the resolution of embracing the strictest religious life; their only hesitation was as to which kind of monastic rule they should adopt—that of the solitary hermit, or that of the monks living in communities. Neither of these, however, was immediately adopted by Gregory, who returned to his father's house, acknowledging the call of filial piety to be stronger than that to the solitary life; a decision rare indeed in chronicles of monkish saints.

While Basil made a tour among the societies of monks who peopled the deserts in Egypt and Syria, and finally retired to a mountain solitude in Pontus, Gregory remained at Nazianzum, and consented, against his natural tastes, to become his father's associate in the bishopric. Letters, playfully contrasting the advantages of solitary and city life, passed between the friends, from some of which it would seem as if a romantic taste for natural beauty mingled with asceticism in their preference for a solitary life. Basil endeavoured to draw Gregory to join him, by a description of his solitude, more like that of a Robinson Crusoe's island than of a stern, penitential hermitage. "There is a lofty mountain," he says, "covered with thick woods, watered towards the north with cool and transparent streams. A plain lies beneath, enriched by the waters which are ever draining off upon it, and skirted by a spontaneous profusion of trees, almost thick enough to be a fence, so as even to surpass Calypso's island, which Homer seems to have thought the most beautiful spot on earth. Indeed, it is like an island, enclosed as it is on all sides; for deep hollows cut off two sides of it; the river, which has lately fallen down a precipice, runs along the front, and is impassable as a wall; while the mountain, extending itself behind, and meeting the hollows in a crescent, stops up the path at its roots. Behind my abode there is another gorge, rising into a ledge above, so as to command the extent of the plain and the stream which bounds it; the most rapid stream I know shooting down over the rocks, and eddying in a deep pool, an inexhaustible resource to the country people in the countless fish which its depths contain." Then he goes on to speak of the multitude of flowers and singing-birds, the breezes and soft mists, the deer and wild goats, and "quietness, the sweetest produce of all."[1] There for a time Gregory visited Basil; and a happy, Robinson Crusoe-like life the friends seem to have led; hewing stones and felling trees for their hermitage; planting vines on the hill-side; resting under the shadow of a golden plane; sweetening the toil with converse full of playful allusions to their college studies; "sharpening their hearts" with religious communion, and in the loving study of the Bible, "finding light with the guidance of the Spirit." With longing heart Gregory afterwards looked back to those quiet days, from his busy city life, recalling, above all, "the psalmodies, and vigils, and departures to God in prayer." He was not, however, to be enticed by any such delights from the home of his aged father and mother; and the sacrifice he thus made was perhaps dearer to God than the sacrifice he longed to make.

Solitude, however, throughout his life continued his one passion, and made its course (as Neander says) a perpetual oscillation. Driven to active life by the necessities of the times, he fled to his beloved retirement whenever he found it possible. In his childhood he had had a dream, in which he saw two virgin forms clothed in fair white raiment; their names were "Purity" and "Sobriety;" they stood by Christ, the King, and they offered, if he would unite his mind to theirs, to carry him aloft to heaven. This dream, he says, he never forgot; a high ideal of the beauty of holiness was before his mind, and, after the fashion of his times, he sought it in the solitude of the monastic life. God,

---

[1] Newman's "Church of the Fathers."

however (as far as we may interpret His will by His providence), chose otherwise for him, and brought him back again and again to the tempestuous sea of life, to the routine of daily intercourse, and the monotonous pressure of ecclesiastical business. We, in the clearer light of distance, may perhaps see that the true discipline was in the life appointed for him, and that the ascetic discipline he sought would have been, in comparison, a weakening self-indulgence. May not the lesson teach many of us a trustful submission, when our own plans and visions are similarly crossed?

Gregory's times were remarkably unquiet: struggles of the sharpest kind were rending both the Church and the world. The outward attacks of Julian the Apostate were, as Gregory himself says, almost a rest, compared with the bitter inward strife of sects and heresies. The Nicene Creed was not yet fixed, and the anatomy of the countless heresies, which sprang up in continually fresh combinations, might occupy a lifetime and yet teach nothing. Besides the divisions occasioned by doctrinal differences, there were perplexing schisms between the partisans of various champions of the same doctrine; so that any attempt to comprehend and remember them all is not merely difficult as the study of a straightforward natural science, but hopeless as the attempt to learn the varying nomenclature of fashionable horticulture. Through all these perplexities, Gregory Nazianzen, Basil the Great, and Gregory of Nyssa, the three Cappadocian fathers, had to wind their way. No wonder that Gregory preferred the honest conflict with the worship of goddesses and idols, to such subtle dissections of what should have been adored, well-nigh destroying the life of the true doctrine in the process of separating it from the false. No wonder that good men turned with a rebounding of the heart from the quarrels of Arians, Semi-Arians, Apollinarians, Eustathians, and Meletians, to quiet mountain solitude and healthy bodily toil, nocturnal psalmodies, and departures of the heart to God. Gregory of Nazianzum's last voyage into the tempestuous sea he so much dreaded, was a glorious one. At fifty years of age he was called to Constantinople, to stem the torrent of Arianism there. The house of one of his relatives was opened to him as a place of worship, all the churches being in Arian hands. Under the Arian Emperor Valens, and in the midst of a populace fanatically opposed to the ancient faith, he preached the absolute Deity of Christ, and sought to bring home the truth to the hearts as well as the intellects of his hearers. He was pelted by the mob, and persecuted by the higher classes, and with difficulty obtained an acquittal from the tribunal before which he was brought on the charge of occasioning a riot. But he preached on; his audience increased, the house in which they met was converted into a church; and to that church, when the victory was at length gained, was given the name of Anastasia, as the place of resurrection of the truth. On the accession of the orthodox Theodosius, Gregory was chosen Patriarch of Constantinople; but, difficulties arising about the appointment, he resigned, and once more retired from public life. His father and mother, his brother and sister, were all dead, and his retirement seems to have been unbroken; and eight years afterwards,—nine years after the death of his friend Basil,—Gregory of Nazianzum died.

The friendship of Gregory and Basil was not uninterrupted. It must be useless in these days to attempt to find out the causes of differences which, probably, neither their contemporaries nor themselves fully understood. As with Paul and Barnabas, their reconciliation is not narrated to us. Probably in this life the broken links were never re-knit; but Gregory preached Basil's funeral eulogy; and we must believe that the division has long since been healed, by one touch of that Hand which was pierced for both. That, with all the other tumults of their lives, has passed away: the discord into which their happy union fell has ages since been drawn up into a higher harmony. The work they tried to do for God has surely not been forgotten; and the great work Christ did for them has, surely, not been in vain. For, as Basil said, "This is the perfect and absolute glorying in God, when a man is not elated by his own righteousness, but knows himself to be wanting in true righteousness, and justified by faith alone, which is in Christ."

It was through the labours, and conflicts, and perplexities of such a life as this, that Gregory wrote his hymns. From the midst of his work in the world, as well as in the quiet of his beloved solitude, doubtless his heart often "departed to God" on the wings of praise. He is said to be rhetorical and over-laboured in his writings; but the following lines are chosen, like all the rest in this volume, as utterances of the Christian life, rather than as specimens of poetical power.

HYMN TO CHRIST.

Daniel, vol. iii. pp. 5, 6. IV.

Hear us now, Eternal Monarch,
Grant us now to hymn and praise Thee—
Thee the King, and Thee the Master!
By whom are our hymns and praises,
By whom are the choirs of angels,
By whom flow the ceaseless ages,
   By whom only shines the sun,
By whom walks the moon in brightness,
By whom smile the stars in beauty,
By whom all the race of mortals
Have received their godlike reason,
   And Thine other works outshone.
Thou the universe createdst,
   Hast to each his place decreed,
Constituting all in wisdom;
   And Thy word, Lord, was a deed.
For Thy word, Son of the Highest,
In essential might and glory,
Equals that of God the Father,
   Who creates and reigns o'er all;
Whilst the Spirit all embraceth,
All preserving, all providing:
   Triune God, on Thee we call.
Thou, the one and only Monarch,
In Thy nature changeless, endless
Of unutterable glory,
Inaccessible in wisdom,

Never-wearied strength of heaven,
Infinite, without beginning,
   High in unapproached light;
All with sleepless eye observing,
Not a depth Thy glance escapeth,
From the earth to the abysses,
   Deepest deep or highest height;
   Wheresoe'er my lot may be,
   Grant me thus to worship Thee.
Cleanse me, Lord, from my transgression,
Purge me from an evil conscience,
That Thy Godhead I may honour;
Holy hands in praise uplifting,
   Blessing Christ on bended knee.
Own me, then, at last Thy servant,
   When Thou com'st in majesty.
Be to me a pitying Father,
Let me find Thy grace and mercy;
And to Thee all praise and glory
   Through the endless ages be.

After the weary toil of the day, and the strife of tongues, Gregory's spirit thus fled to the secret tabernacle, into which the empty noises of earth cannot penetrate, the pavilion of the presence of God:—

EVENING HYMN.

Daniel, vol. iii. p. 13. XIII.

Christ, my Lord, I come to bless Thee,
   Now when day is veil'd in night
Thou who knowest no beginning,
   Light of the Eternal Light.

Thou the darkness hast dissolvèd,
And the outward light created,
   That all things in light might be;
Fixing the unfixed chaos,
Moulding it to wondrous beauty,
   Into the fair world we see.

Thou enlight'nest man with reason,
   Far beyond the creatures dumb;
That light in thy light beholding,
   Wholly light he might become.

Thou hast set the radiant heavens
With Thy many lamps of brightness,
   Filling all the vaults above,
Day and night in turn subjecting
To a brotherhood of service
   And a mutual law of love;

By the night our wearied nature
   Resting from its toils and tears;
To the works, Lord, that thou lovest,
   Waking us when day appears.

Again, in another hymn to Christ, his soul flees with its burden of sins direct to that Refuge, where the weary and heavy laden find rest. Some of its expressions of deep self-despair and trembling trust may be thus rendered:—

Daniel, vol. iii. p. 13. XLI. 5.

Unfruitful, sinful, bearing weeds and thorns,
   Fruits of the curse, ah! whither shall I flee?
O Christ, most blessed, bid my fleeting days
   Flow heavenward! Christ, sole fount of hope to me!

The enemy is near; to Thee I cling!
   Strengthen, oh strengthen me by might Divine;
Let not the trembling bird be from Thine altar driven!
   Save me, it is Thy will, O Christ! save me, for I am
      Thine!

One other hymn of Gregory's may be given, at least in part. It is a voice from those eight years which he spent in retirement, when his work was done, the Church of the Anastasia had arisen, and father, mother, brother, and sister, all were dead. In the depths of its natural fears, and the firmness of the hope to which at last it rises, it tells the history of those solitary years, and echoes well the music of those ancient psalms, which soar so often "out of the depths" into the light of God.

TO HIMSELF.

Daniel, vol. iii. p. 11. x.

Where are the wingèd words? Lost in the air.
   Where the fresh flower of youth and glory? Gone.
The strength of well-knit limbs? Brought low by care.
   Wealth? Plunder'd; none possess but God alone.
Where those dear parents who my life first gave,
And where that holy twain, brother and sister? In the
     grave.

My fatherland alone to me is left,
   And heaving factions flood my country o'er;
Thus, with uncertain steps, of all bereft,
   Exiled and homeless, childless, aged, poor,
No child mine age to soothe with service sweet,
I live from day to day with ever-wandering feet.

What lies before me? Where shall set my day?
   Where shall these weary limbs at length repose?
What hospitable tomb receive my clay?
   What hands at last my failing eyes shall close?
What eyes will watch me?—Eyes with pity fraught?
Some friend of Christ? Or those who know Him not?

Or shall no tomb, as in a casket, lock
   This frame, when laid a weight of breathless clay?
Cast forth unburied on the desert rock,
   Or thrown in scorn to birds and beasts of prey;
Consumed and cast in handfuls on the air,
Left in some river-bed to perish there?

This as Thou wilt: the Day will all unite
   Wherever scatter'd, when Thy word is said:
Rivers of fire, abysses without light,
   Thy great tribunal,—these alone are dread.
And Thou, O Christ, my King, art fatherland to me!
Strength, wealth, eternal rest, yea, all I find in Thee!

Thus, in the old Ionic tongue, the wail of feeble mortality went forth once more, but with a close the old Ionic music never knew; for Christ had died, and risen from the dead, and the other world was a region of melancholy voiceless shades no longer; for He is there.

No wonder that when that chord of hope had once been struck, no effort of an apostate emperor, no refinement of pagan art or philosophy, could silence it; for, with all its beauty, if the old music once ceased to be Bacchanalian, what could it end in but a death wail?

A few more Christian hymns reach us from the East, lingering on even after the religion of Mohammed had started on its fiery course, beginning, as it did, in the devastation of a flood of fire, and ending in its ashes, having for its sacred music but the battle cry and the funeral wail. About the sacred poems of Cosmas the Hierosolymite, there is a majestic music. They seem to march solemnly, as if in battle array, recurring at intervals to a grand refrain, as if meant to be taken up in chorus. The words are such as these. In a hymn on the Nativity, the choral words recur continually—

> That He might be glorified.

Then again—

> Glory to Thy power, O Lord,—
> God of our fathers, blessed art Thou.

Again—

> Let all creation bless the Lord,
> And glorify Thy name from age to age.

In a hymn on the Epiphany the varying refrains are—

> That He might be glorified.

Then at regular intervals—

> For Thou art Christ, wisdom and power of God.

And again—

> Peace, passing understanding, Thou bestowest.

And—

> Spare Thou our souls and save us, Christ our God.

It is difficult to give the music of these recurring strains in a translation, and the hymns are long;

but the effect must surely have been very impressive, and one would like to know the music to which they were sung, unless indeed the measure was the music. Andrew of Crete, and John the Damascene, continued yet further to prolong the song of the Eastern Church, whilst the terrible flood was gathering in Arabia, which was so soon to sweep over Christendom, and altogether to desolate and submerge its Eastern half. But before that sacred music was silenced, its tone had long begun to ring less clear. Invocations to the Mother of God, "the all-holy," crowd thicker and thicker on those later hymns; and if Mohammedanism had not broken all the strings at once, there seems a danger that they would have fallen of themselves into more and more jarring discord. Perhaps the very agony of that great desolation tuned many a heart to a music it had not known before.

Some things may be deficient in these early Oriental hymns; we might wish to see the Cross and redeeming death of Christ more their centre, as it was St. Paul's; but until the fourth century, we must remember, the Christian Church was singing her song in the midst of a heathen world. Her enemies knew that she worshipped One who had been crucified; and while she boldly confessed the fact, and contentedly endured all the scorn it drew on her, her natural desire was to honour, with every venerable title, Him whom the world thus rejected and despised. Jew and Gentile knew that Jesus had been crucified: the Church knew that He had risen, and was indeed Christ the

King. It is, perhaps, therefore natural that the earliest hymns should have dwelt rather on the glories visible only to faith, than on the humiliation which was evident to the eye of flesh; and thus the Good Shepherd and the Vine rather than the Cross, the symbols of victory and peace and life rather than those of death and shame and strife, are found in the earliest Catacombs where the persecuted Christians, themselves daily exposed to perils of shame and torture and death, were laid to rest. The tribulation was in their life, and they needed in their religion symbols of victory and joy.

It is in contrasting the early Christian hymns with heathen poetry, that their beauty and truth would probably be most manifest. The faith that could bear to look at death, because looking through it, the gaze into the spiritual world, the hope and love and peace, and above all, the adoring, trusting contemplation of that Glorious Person, divine and human, who had so lately come to earth, and so lately left it,—it is this which gives their beauty to the Oriental hymns. They are full of that living Saviour, Jesus, son of Mary and Son of God; the Almighty God stooping for our sakes to become the infant of days, hymned by angels, and worshipped by magi and shepherds; the Lamb of God taking away the sin of the world; the suffering Redeemer stretching His hands on the cross to rescue the lost, by the cross recovering what Adam had forfeited; the mighty Victor, by death trampling on death, and by His resurrection opening to us the gates of life; now ascended in triumph to heaven, yet undivided from His own;

merciful, holy, loving Man, Friend, Master, King, Saviour, Redeeming Sufferer, Infinite and Omnipotent Son of God.

These hymns are indeed inspired by love of the victorious Saviour and sung to Him; and if, like birds at the dawn, all their music reaches only this one strain, "The Sun has risen," is it not enough? For all other truths shine only in the light of this truth, and all other true joys flow only from this fountain. The Sun will bring the summer. No wonder that when first that Sun arose, the disciples could say little to one another, but "The Lord is risen indeed."

CHAPTER V

ST. AMBROSE AND THE AMBROSIAN HYMNS

WE have now reached a third stage in the history of Christian hymns. The inspired songs, recorded by inspired men, were succeeded by uninspired hymns. Yet the language remained the same as that of the inspired books. The hosannas of Ephrem the Syrian had the sound as well as the sense of those of the children of Jerusalem, and both were sung in a dialect kindred to that in which Israel first chanted the song of Moses by the Red Sea. Clement of Alexandria, Gregory of Nazianzum, and the unknown earliest singers of the Oriental Churches, thought in the very words of evangelists and apostles; the phrases of the New Testament were literally their household words. Sacred song had not yet passed away from the two original sacred languages; but now a new language was to be consecrated. The stream of psalmody was to flow from the tongue of Homer, Plato, and the New Testament, into that of Virgil, Cicero, and the Vulgate; the ecclesiastical language of so many centuries had to be moulded out of the sonorous old Roman speech.

The Latin hymns of the fourth and fifth centuries form quite a distinct school. They stand between the old world and the new; between the refinements of the ancient classical literature, and those who only knew Latin as an ecclesiastical or foreign language; between Greek and Gothic art; between the ancient Pagan civilization, and that new Christian civilization which was to rise at length to light after its long underground course in the Middle Ages. Their form links them with the old and their substance with the new dynasty. They cling to the old rhythm, although in its least elaborate shape, and never descend to the barbarism of rhyme.

They are, perhaps, deficient in some qualities which severally shine in earlier and later Christian poetry. Compared with those of the Greek Church, they read rather like translations. And in a sense are they not translations? The wonderful flexibility of the Greek language adapted itself at once to the new flood of thought which had to pass into it. The delicacy of its subtle shades of meaning; the thunder and lightning of those single words which flash the power of a sentence on you in a moment, condensing the force of a phrase on a point; its endless reproductive faculty;—all these had been fused for centuries in the furnace of democratic assemblies, delicately moulded by the subtlest philosophical intellects, fitted for every-day purposes by the constant use of a witty, lively, highly-educated people, when at length the men came who were to wield the perfect weapon for God and humanity. And the process of preparation was completed by the Divine hand. The truths of Christianity flowed for the first time, in Greek, from inspired lips.

With Latin it was quite different. The mighty new thought had to be fitted into the comparatively stiff and narrow mould of Roman speech, and the hands which were to accomplish the work were not those of apostles and evangelists.

Again : in comparing the early Latin hymns with those of the Middle Ages, there is perhaps one disadvantage on the side of the earlier. In the days of Ambrose, the language had not gathered around it the spiritual and ecclesiastical associations of centuries. It had to come into the Church fresh from the market, the battle-field, or the court of justice, with no sacred laver of inspiration to baptize it from the stains and dust of secular or sinful employment; though this indeed has its advantage in not substituting technical religious phraseology for the true speech of common life.

And there is a calm and steady glow in these early Latin hymns, a straightforward plainness of speech, and an unconscious force, which grow on you wonderfully as you become more acquainted with them. If they have not the sublime simplicity of a faith which sees visions, and leaves it to fancy to scatter flowers, or the fervency of an outburst of solitary devotion, the regular beauty of Greek art, or the imaginative depth and homely pathos of Teutonic sacred ballads, they have a Roman majesty of their own, the majesty of a national anthem, the subdued fire of the battle-song of a disciplined army. The imperial dignity of the great language of law and of war has passed into them; they are the grand national anthems of the Church militant, and their practical plainness, their healthy objective life, are bracing as mountain air.

Four names are especially associated with the Latin hymnology of what may be called the Ambrosian period; those of Ambrose, Augustine, Hilary, and Prudentius.

Aurelius Prudentius Clemens was a Roman of good family, a native of northern Spain; he was born A.D. 348. The old classical Latin was still living then, and was his mother tongue; the old paganism was not yet dead, the altar to the goddess of Victory was in the Senate House, the Vestal Virgins still held their revenues from the State, when he visited the tombs of the Christian martyrs in the catacombs at Rome. But his own faith in the power of the victorious living Christ was so strong, that the dispossessed gods to him had become mere dreams of the night, and he would fearlessly have preserved these statues for their beauty as works of art. A loyal Roman, full of confidence that the conquests of the Empire would be conquests of Christianity, he held high civil office. But late in life, moved by a deep religious impression, he abandoned all secular offices and dignities and devoted himself to prayer and sacred poetry, "offering his verses to Christ" as the "earthen vessel" of a "rustic poet." Some of the titles of his writings are full of high spiritual meaning. "The true Temple," "The true Worship," "The true Fast," "The true Nobility," "The true Reward," "The true Riches." He was the great Christian poet of those early centuries, the author of their "Christian Year," and of their popular morning and evening hymns. Those translated here are a Funeral Hymn and a Hymn on the Epiphany.

Hilary, Metropolitan of Arles, author of the Hymns, in his youth sold his estates, and gave the proceeds to the poor, devoting himself to a religious life in the monastery of Lerins. From Lerins he was called to the Bishopric of Arles. As Bishop he went on foot throughout his diocese, when in his episcopal city living like St. Augustine in a community of clergy. He had a severe conflict with St. Leo of Rome about the rights of the Metropolitan See of Arles.

St. Leo speaks of him after his death as a man of holy memory; to him belongs the fine saying, "Peace also has its martyrs."

He died at the age of forty-nine, with a reputation which made it possible to attribute to him one of the three great Creeds, and one of the three great Hymns, the Athanasian Creed, and the "Te Deum."

Ambrose, whose name defines the Hymns of his age, stands before us in himself a complete historical picture, a representative portrait of his times, although revealed to us rather as an historical personage than in his inner history as a man, and a brother in the great Christian family.

Augustine's spiritual history has probably had

more influence on the Christian life of fifteen centuries, than the history of any other human being except St. Paul. He is one of the very few men of past times whose heart we seem to know; whose writings are not preached to us from the pulpit of history, but spoken in the voice of a friend.

The biographies of Ambrose and Augustine might be combined into a complete compendium of the ecclesiastical history of their times, the one reflecting its more external features, and the other its inward spiritual conflicts; Ambrose representing the relations between Church and State, bishops and emperors, and Augustine the relation between the soul and truth.

In one sense, all periods are periods of transition; no social forms can be permanent; and when men imagine a point attained, and a fixed state of law and society reached, even while they contemplate their work it is changing into something else. But the fourth century was peculiarly and visibly an age of transition. The new Gothic element had appeared in the world, and it had yet to be proved whether the strong Northern races would be smoothed down and fitted into the old imperial polity, or whether they would spread and prevail, until the relics of the former civilization would be glad to shelter themselves under their broad shadow. All kinds of heterogeneous materials lay unshapen beside each other in those days. Whilst the clergy and even the mobs of the East were disputing about the minutest distinctions of the Christian creed, and the banner of the Cross had become the standard of the empire, the Roman senate was still holding its shadowy sessions under the tutelage of the goddess of Victory. It was not till the latter half of the century that the old Pagan rites were discontinued as a part of state ceremonies, although Paganism must long have ceased to be a national faith, and had probably as little to do with the religion of the people of Rome then, as the Lord Mayor's Show with the civil or commercial rights of England now. The ghost of the old Roman senate and the ghost of the old Roman religion found a fitting companionship in each other.

Temples still stood, relics of ancient art, and perhaps, in great anxieties, still the refuge of some passionate hearts, who would fain rend their requests from Heaven; but the monks and the populace were rapidly sweeping them away. Yet, unhappily, the old idolatry had not passed away. Those who sought from Heaven merely the fulfilment of earthly wishes, were provided with a host of intercessors and mediators, already scarcely less numerous than the dwellers on Olympus. The sacred dust of martyrs was no longer suffered to rest in peace till the resurrection, but, as Vigilantius complained, and Jerome angrily admitted, was carried reverently about in little urns. So little did some who bore the name of Christ apprehend His love, that they deemed the lifeless remains of His disciples a surer safeguard than His living providence, perhaps even (unconsciously) a shield against His purposes.

Meantime the Arian controversy raged fiercely

in the East and West. The Gothic soldiers, who had been introduced into the imperial armies and palaces, however little they knew of the subject, warmly espoused the quarrel. If they could not reason, at least they could fight, and thus claim their share in the Church history of the times.

The monastic rule was more and more becoming the highest ideal of religious life. The course of Christian life was in too many instances stiffened from the river into the canal, flowing, not amidst fruitful meadows, which it fertilized, but between rigid stone walls, which it could only wear away; and too often it was ponded back into stagnant isolation. From such monastic retirement came, indeed, at times, fervent hymns, such as those of Gregory of Nazianzum; tender, childlike poems, such as those of Ephrem Syrus; and works of universal beneficence, such as Jerome's Vulgate. Doubtless, also, many a shipwrecked heart found a haven there, and many a child, orphaned by war, shelter and care. For when God gives eternal life it is strong, and struggles through inconceivable obstacles to fulfil its work of blessing, and "God fulfils Himself in many ways."

In the midst of such an age as this, Ambrose of Milan grew to manhood. He was of a noble Roman family, in days when the patricians of Rome still traced back their pedigree to times before the Cæsars. His father was prefect of Gaul, and Trèves and Arles contend for the honour of being his birth-place. Before the age of thirty, he himself became Consular of Liguria, and resided at the imperial city of Milan. Ecclesiastical honours could scarcely, therefore, to him have been objects of secular ambition, however he may have esteemed them as weapons of spiritual warfare.

The circumstances which led to his appointment to the bishopric of Milan throw a strange light on many questions of Church history. The long contest for supremacy between the clergy and the empire had hardly yet commenced; and when Auxentius, the Arian bishop of Milan, died, the citizens of Milan and the Emperor Valentinian I. endeavoured to throw on each other the perilous responsibility of choosing his successor. The perplexing privilege reverted finally to the people. The city was thrown into tumult, and the cathedral was filled by a noisy and excited multitude. In the midst of the storm Ambrose appeared as civil governor, and commanded peace. In the temporary lull which followed his entrance, a child's voice arose, shouting, "Ambrose is bishop!" The whole multitude, seized by a sudden sympathetic impulse, responded, "Ambrose is bishop! Ambrose is bishop!" And so, after some weeks of hesitation and resistance, Ambrose became bishop. To Ambrose the episcopate was no haven of repose, but a sphere of earnest conflict for truth and right. In the two great contests with the imperial court which signalize his life, the people were heartily with him.

His first conflict was for doctrine; for the preservation of the Catholic Creed against the Arians. He refused to yield up the Portian Basilica to the Empress Justina for the use of the Arians. The churches, he said, were not the bishop's, but Christ's; and the bishop, as His steward, could not relinquish them without treachery, to those who denied His Deity. He said, and no doubt he felt, it was better for him to be deposed or put to death. He would use no earthly weapons. Excommunication he believed to be a spiritual weapon, and he launched it at the soldiers who should dare to seize the building. Passive resistance he deemed it right to carry to the utmost extent. The mass of the people of Milan, rich and poor, were strongly opposed to Arianism, and at length they took possession of the disputed basilica and the range of buildings connected with it, by quietly filling them. The imperial troops besieged them there during many days, making no attack, but not suffering any to leave the church, hoping to exhaust the patience of which crowds have usually such a scanty stock. Then first, it is said, was introduced into the Western Church responsive chanting of hymns long prevalent in the Eastern Churches, used by Chrysostom during vigils, and by the Christians of Antioch as a weapon against heresy. The hymns of Ambrose resounded through the basilica, and the city was his choir.

No doubt the words had long been familiar to the people of Milan. Ambrose says in one of his sermons, "They say the people are misled by the verses of my hymns. I frankly confess this also. Truly they have in them a high strain, above all other influence. For can any strain have more of influence than the confession of the Holy Trinity, which is proclaimed day by day by the voice of the whole people? Each is eager to rival his fellows in confessing, as he well knows how, in sacred verses, his faith in Father, Son, and Holy Spirit. Thus all are made teachers who else were scarce equal to being scholars."

Monica, St. Augustine's mother, was among that multitude who gathered around the bishop. The contest was for no trifling point. We are apt to throw back on this scene the shadow of the after struggle between the Papacy and the Empire, when Hildebrand kept the humbled emperor shivering in penance amongst the snows at Canossa. But the conflict in the days of Ambrose was for an integral part of the Creed, and his weapon was patient endurance. That the Creed St. Ambrose thus contended for was no mere lifeless theological subtlety, is proved by the nature of his second contest with the imperial court, when he enforced a public confession and penance on the orthodox emperor Theodosius the Great, for his crime in commanding a revengeful and treacherous massacre of thousands of the citizens of Thessalonica. Truth and right, moral and religious truth, were not divorced in his mind.

These stormy scenes passed away, but the Church psalmody which had sprung from the conflict retained its hold on the hearts of the people, and retained also the masculine vigour and militant austerity which became its birth. Thus the hymns of the Western Church were cradled on the battlefield, and the sublime strains of faith which are now chanted in Latin in Europe by priests and choristers, were once the household hymns of the people.

St. Augustine can hardly be numbered among the hymn writers; the one hymn attributed to him, and frequently introduced amongst his works, is said to have been written six centuries later by Cardinal Damiani. He speaks of himself in his "Confessions" as having "indited verses," but that was before his conversion. Yet, as one of the mightiest instruments in fitting the Latin language to spiritual uses, and as the great channel through which the doctrines of grace flowed to the Middle Ages, and thus, doubtless, the source of many hymns, his name should scarcely be omitted among the number of those by whom the sacred song was uttered. Many passages of his "Confessions" are full of the richest melody of the heart; indeed, are not the whole of the "Confessions," with their constant "departing of the heart to God," one continuous hymn, one constant ascending of the soul from the creature to the Creator, from self to the Saviour?

The chief link, however, which binds the name of Augustine to our subject, is his record of the impression made by these early Latin hymns on his own heart. He says (Conf., b. ix. 14, 15):—

"Nor was I sated in those days with the wondrous sweetness of considering the depth of Thy counsels concerning the salvation of mankind. How did I weep, through Thy hymns and canticles touched to the quick by the voices of Thy sweet attuned Church! The voices sank into mine ears, and the truth distilled into mine heart, whence the affections of my devotions overflowed; tears ran down, and happy was I therein.

"Not long had the Church of Milan begun to use this kind of consultation and exhortation, the brethren zealously joining with harmony of voice and heart. For it was a year, or not much more, that Justina, mother to the Emperor Valentinian, then a child, persecuted Thy servant Ambrose, in favour of her heresy to which she was seduced by the Arians. The devout people kept watch in the church, ready to die with their bishop, Thy servant. There my mother, Thy handmaid, bearing a chief part in those anxieties and watchings, lived for prayer. We, yet unwarmed by the heat of Thy Spirit, still were stirred up by the sight of the amazed and disquieted city. Then it was instituted that, after the manner of the Eastern Churches, hymns and psalms should be sung, lest the people should wax faint through the tediousness of sorrow; and from that day to this the custom is retained, divers (yea, almost all) Thy congregations throughout other parts of the world following herein."

Another passage (in the 9th book) is especially valuable, as showing the power of those Latin hymns, which seem to us rather majestic than soothing, to speak comfort to Christian mourners in those days. Their healing virtue must have lain in their truth. Speaking of the death of that mother who had watched him through all his wanderings, with such patient love, hoping against hope, he writes:—

"I closed her eyes, and there flowed withal a mighty sorrow into my heart, which was overflowing into tears; mine eyes, at the same time, by the violent command of my mind, drank up their fountain wholly dry, and woe was me in such a strife! But when she breathed her last, the boy Adeodatus (Augustine's son) burst into a loud lament; then, checked by us all, held his peace. In like manner, also, a childish feeling in me, which was, through my heart's youthful voice, finding its vent in weeping, was checked and silenced. For we thought it not fitting to solemnize that funeral with fearful lament and groanings: for thereby do they, for the most part, express the grief for the departed, as though unhappy or altogether dead; whereas she was neither unhappy in her death, nor altogether dead. Of this we were assured on good grounds; the testimony of her good conversation, and her faith unfeigned. What, then, was it which did grievously pain me within, but a fresh wound wrought through the sudden wrench of that most sweet and dear custom of living together? I joyed in her testimony, when, in that her last sickness, mingling her endearment with my acts of duty, she called me 'dutiful,' and mentioned, with great affection of love, that she never had heard any harsh or reproachful sound uttered by my mouth against her. But yet, O my God, who madest us, what comparison is there between that honour that I paid to her, and her slavery for me? Being, then, forsaken of so great comfort in her, my soul was wounded, and that life rent asunder, as it were, which of hers and mine together had been made but one.

"The boy Adeodatus then being stilled from weeping, Euodius took up the Psalter, and began to sing (our whole house answering him) the psalm— 'I will sing of mercy and judgment; to thee, O Lord, will I sing.' But hearing what we were doing, many brethren and religious women came together; and whilst they whose office it was made ready for the burial, as the manner is, I, in a part of the house where I might properly, together with those who thought not fit to leave me, discoursed upon something fitting the time; and by this balm of truth assuaged that torment, known to Thee, they unknowing and listening intently, and conceiving me to be without all sense of sorrow. But in Thy ears, where none of them heard, I blamed the weakness of my feelings, and refrained my flood of grief, which gave way a little unto me, but again came, as with a tide, yet not so as to burst out into tears, nor to a change of countenance; still I knew what I was keeping down in my grief."

And after her burial, he continues:—

"Nor did I weep even at those prayers; yet was I the whole day heavily sad, and with troubled mind prayed Thee, as I could, to heal my sorrow; yet Thou didst not; impressing, I believe, on my memory by this one instance, how strong the bond of habit is even on a soul which now feeds on no deceiving word."

Then he tried to refresh himself with bathing:—

"But the bitterness of sorrow," he continues, "could not thus be washed from my heart. Then I slept, and woke up again, and found my grief not a little softened; and, as I was alone in my bed, I remembered those true verses of Thine Ambrose:—

'Maker of all, the Lord
And Ruler of the height,

> Who, robing day in light, hast pour'd
> Soft slumbers o'er the night;
> That to our limbs the power
> Of toil may be renew'd,
> And hearts be raised that sink and cower,
> And sorrows be subdued.'[1]

"And then, by little and little, I recovered my former thoughts of Thy handmaid, her holy conversation towards Thee, her holy tenderness and consideration towards us, whereof I was suddenly deprived; and I was minded to weep in Thy sight for her and for myself, in her behalf and on my own. And I gave way to the tears which before I restrained, to overflow as much as they desired, reposing my heart upon them; and it found rest in them, for it was in Thine ears, not in those of men, who would have scornfully interpreted my weeping. And now, Lord, in writing, I confess it unto Thee. Read it who will and interpret it how he will; and if he finds sin therein that I wept my mother for a small portion of an hour (the mother who, for the time, was dead to mine eyes, who had for many years wept for me, that I might live in Thine eyes), let him not deride me; but rather, if he be one of large charity, let him weep himself for my sins unto Thee, the Father of all the brethren of Thy Christ."

Thus did those early Latin hymns speak to the men of their times. It is interesting thus to trace them home from the great congregation to the

---

[1] Thus translated in "Confession of St. Augustine." Oxford: John Henry Parker, 1848. The whole of the original hymn has been translated afresh, and is given at the end of the chapter.

mourner's solitary heart. In the 10th book of his "Confessions," Augustine speaks of his perplexity in defining the limits of the use of church music in devotion, fearing that the senses might thus be more delighted than the heart really raised to God. The whole passage must be quoted to explain his feelings in this instance, also representing, doubtless, the perplexities of many in his own time, as well as in ours :—

"The delights of the ear," he writes, "had more firmly entangled and subdued me; but Thou didst loosen and free me. Now in those melodies which Thy words breathe soul into, when sung with a sweet and attuned voice, I do a little repose, yet not so as to be held thereby but that I can disengage myself when I will. But with the words, which are their life, and whereby they find admission into me, themselves seek in my affections a place of some estimation; and I can scarcely assign them one suitable. For at one time I seem to myself to give them more honour than is seemly, feeling our minds to be more holily and fervently raised into a flame of devotion by the holy words themselves when thus sung, than when not; and that the several affections of our spirit, by a sweet variety, have their own proper measures in the voice and singing, by some hidden correspondence wherewith they are stirred up. But this contentment of the flesh, to which the soul must not be given over to be enervated, doth oft beguile me, the sense not so waiting upon reason as patiently to follow her; but having been admitted merely for her sake it strives even to run before her and lead her. Thus in these things I unawares sin, but afterwards am aware of it.

"At other times, shunning over anxiously this very deception, I err in too great strictness, and sometimes to that degree as to wish the whole melody of sweet music which is used in David's Psalter banished from my ears, and the Church's too; and that mode seems to me safer which I remember to have been often told me of Athanasius, bishop of Alexandria, who made the reader of the psalm utter it with so slight an inflection of voice that it was nearer speaking than singing. Yet again, when I remember the tears I shed in the psalmody of Thy Church, in the beginning of my recovered faith, and how at this time I am moved, not with the singing, but with the things sung, when they are sung with a clear voice and modulation most suitable, I acknowledge the great use of this institution. Thus I fluctuate between peril and pleasure, and approved wholesomeness; inclined the rather (though not as pronouncing an irrevocable opinion) to approve of the usage of singing in the church, that so by the delight of the ears the weaker minds may rise to the feelings of devotion. Yet, when it befalls me to be more moved with the voice than with the words sung, I confess to have sinned penally, and then had rather not hear music. See now my state: weep with me, and weep for me, ye who so regulate your feelings within as that good action follows. For you who do not act, these things touch not you. But Thou, O Lord my God, hearken, behold, and see, and have mercy and heal me, Thou in whose presence I have become a problem to myself; and that is my infirmity."

Such was the conflict in St. Austin's mind, which afterwards found a broad battle-field in Christendom: the great debate whether art more tends to draw our whole mixed nature heavenwards, or to draw the soul earthwards. With regard to music in psalms, and hymns, and spiritual songs, the question seems to be settled in the same all-penetrating pages where it is written, "Every creature of God is good, and to be received with thanksgiving." Nevertheless, the relations of the hymns and church music of his day to a heart and spirit like Augustine's, must have a deep personal interest for us. The words of those early Western hymns seem borne back to us in a melodious echo from the heart of Augustine.

The character of these early Latin hymns is either objective or occasional. They are inspired by the great objects of the faith, rather than by inward emotions. They are designed for the various ecclesiastical hours (prime, lauds, matins, terce, mid-day, nones, vespers, compline, or midnight), or the several days of the week, and seasons of the Christian year, recalling the events in sacred history which characterize each hour, day, or season.

Sunrise and sunset form naturally the prevailing images of the morning and evening hymns. Christ, the Sun of Righteousness that never sets, the Light that never fades, in Himself at once Day and Light, is their great theme. The hymns called Ambrosian are all in one short iambic measure, in itself a monotonous one, and are unrhymed. Their music must have depended on their being rather sung than said, and the melody must have melted them into the heart. Only a few of them are believed to have been written by St. Ambrose himself.

Whilst undisguised Paganism still lingered in Christendom, and Bibles were scarce and readers rare, there was a beautiful and practical meaning in linking the passing hours with heaven, thus making Time himself read aloud the Gospel history and converting the seasons of the year into a kind of pictorial Bible for the poor. For it must always be remembered that the early Latin hymns were no mere recreations of monastic literary retirement, but sacred popular songs, in a language probably as little varying from the common speech of the people then, as the book Italian of to-day from the various spoken dialects of Milan, Genoa, and Venice. They were not merely read by priests out of missals, or chanted by elaborate choirs in cathedrals; but, as St. Ambrose and St. Augustine tell us, were murmured by the people at their work and in their homes, and sung in grand choruses in the great congregation. These sacred songs, in which the Milanese of those days "rivalled one another in chanting the praises of the Blessed Trinity," are no bare and dry statements of opinion, no mere fierce party-cry, nor, as with the later monks, an ingenious mosaic of subtle distinctions, or a clever compendium of a difficult science. They were earnest, simple, fervent prayers and thanksgivings to God their Father, God their Redeemer, perfect in sympathizing humanity and infinite Deity, and God their Comforter, Three Persons in one incomprehensible but most gracious Godhead. Christ was to those who sang them, not only the Eternal Light of Light, the co-equal Son of the Father, but their Sun and their Shield.

The first four hymns here translated may help us to be present at the devotions of our brethren fourteen hundred years ago, at morning, evening, mid-day, and midnight. The first of which a translation is attempted is the one which in the original shed such peace on St. Augustine's sorrowful heart on the morning after his mother's death. He speaks of it as the composition of St. Ambrose himself. There is certainly something most practical and beautiful in connecting, as this hymn does, the return of morning with that look with which the Lord turned and looked on Peter.

HYMN AT THE COCK-CROWING.

Daniel, vol. i. p. 15. XI.

(*Æterne rerum Conditor.*)

Eternal Maker of the world,
   Who rulest both the night and day,
With order'd times dividing Time,
   Our toil and sorrow to allay.

The watchful herald of the dawn
   Announces day with trumpet shrill;
Lamp to the wayfarer at night,
   Night from itself dividing still.

The morning star arising bright
   Dissolves the darkness from the sky;

And, startled from their baleful schemes,
　　The armed powers of darkness fly.

The mariner re-knits his strength;
　　The stormy sea is lull'd to sleep;
And Peter, called the Church's Rock,[1]
　　Hearing this sound, his sin doth weep.

To strenuous labour let us rise;
　　The cock calls those who slumb'ring lie,
Awakes the sluggard from his couch,
　　Convicts who would their Lord deny.

At the cock-crowing, hope returns,
　　New health through suff'ring bodies flows,
The midnight thief his weapon hides,
　　New faith in sinking spirits glows.

Jesus! upon the falling look,
　　And, looking, heal us, Lord, we pray;
For at Thy look the fallen rise,
　　And guilt in tears dissolves away.

Do Thou, our Light, illume our sense,
　　Do Thou our minds from slumber free;
For Thee our voices first proclaim,
　　And with our lips we sing to Thee.

ST. HILARY'S MORNING HYMN.

Daniel, vol. i. p. 1. 1.

(*Lucis Largitor splendide.*)

Thou bounteous Giver of the light,
　　All-glorious, in whose light serene,

---

[1] Dean Trench, in his "Sacred Latin Poetry," says, with reference to this line, that St. Ambrose elsewhere explains this Rock of the Church to be, "not the flesh, but the faith of Peter."

Now that the night has pass'd away,
    The day pours back her sunny sheen.

Thou art the world's true Morning Star,
    Not that which on the edge of night,
Faint herald of a little orb,
    Shines with a dim and narrow light.

Far brighter than our earthly sun,
    Thyself at once the Light and Day,
The inmost chambers of the heart
    Illumining with heavenly ray.

Thou Radiance of the Father's light,
    Draw near, Creator Thou of all;
The fears of whose removèd grace
    Our hearts with direst dread appal.

And may Thy Spirit fill our souls,
    That in the common needs of time,
In converse with our fellow-men,
    We may be free from every crime.

Be every evil lust repell'd
    By guard of inward purity,
That the pure body evermore
    The Spirit's holy shrine may be.

These are our votive offerings,
    This hope inspires us as we pray,
That this our holy matin light
    May guide us through the busy day.

EVENING HYMN.

Daniel, vol. i. p. 33. XXIII.

(*Christe, qui Lux es et Dies.*)

Christ, who art both our Light and Day,
Shine with Thy face the night away;
For very Light of Light Thou art,
Who doth most blessed light impart.

We pray Thee, O most holy Lord,
Defence to us this night afford;
With quiet let these hours be blest,
And calm in Thee, Lord, be our rest.

No heavy sleep o'er us prevail,
Nor us our deadly foe assail;
Nor by our flesh, through him beguiled,
Be before Thee the soul defiled.

Sleep on our eyes its hold must take,
But let our hearts to Thee awake;
And let Thine own right hand defend
Thy servants who on Thee depend.

Thy servants, purchased with Thy blood,
Yet burden'd with their mortal load,
Remember, Lord! be present here;
Defender of the soul! be near.

MID-DAY HYMN.

Daniel, vol. i. p. 40. XXVIII.

(*Jam sexta sensim solvitur.*)

With silent step we see to-day
The noontide hour before us glide;

Day, poised upon her course midway,
Looks to the night on either side.

Ye faithful servants, be not dumb;
With suppliant hearts and voices come,
The name of God with songs to greet—
The Blessed Name with praises meet.

For, lo! the hour is come again
When sentenced once by mortal men
The Judge of all was doom'd to die,
And on the cross was lifted high.

A sudden horror paled the sun
To see that matchless crime begun;
Swift from that impious day he flies,
And o'er the earth the death-pall lies.

The ancient Foe retains his guile,
Meets every hour with force or wile;
But we, with love to Jesus due,
And holy fear, his ranks press through.

Thus, suppliant, we the Father own,
Together with the King, the Son,
And Holy Ghost, one Trinity;
With lowly hearts beseeching Thee,

That whom he suffer'd to redeem
When thus the noontide hour grew dim,
Again in glory now array'd,
His intercession still may aid.

MIDNIGHT HYMN.

Daniel, vol. i. p. 42. XXXI.

(*Media noctis tempus est.*)

It is the midnight hour,
   Prophetic voices warn;
To Father and to Son once more
   Now be our praise upborne;

And to the Paraclete,—
   The perfect Trinity,
God in one substance infinite,
   Ceaseless our praise should be.

Terror possess'd this hour
   When once the angel sped
Through Egypt with destroying power,
   And the first-born lay dead.

This hour redemption bore
   Peace to the sons of God;
The angel pass'd their threshold o'er,
   Knowing the sign of blood.

From Egypt's weeping voice
   Burst forth the bitter cry;
Israel alone could then rejoice,
   For the Lamb's sake pass'd by.

We are Thine Israël;
   We joy in Thee, O God!
And we the ancient Foe repel,
   Redeem'd by Christ's own blood.

At midnight bursts the cry,
   So saith the evangelist,
"Arise! the Bridegroom draweth nigh,
   The King of Heaven, the Christ."

The virgins then, the wise,
   Go forth their Lord to meet;
Bearing their radiant lamps, they rise,
   Then is their joy complete.

The foolish virgins sleep,
   They seek for light too late;
In vain they knock, and call, and weep,
   Closed is the palace gate.

Let us keep steadfast guard
   With lighted hearts all night,
That, when He comes, we stand prepared,
   And meet Him with delight.

At midnight's season chill
   Lay Paul and Silas bound;
Bound, and in prison, sang they still,
   And, singing, freedom found.

Our prison is this earth,
   And yet we sing to Thee!
Break sin's strong fetters, lead us forth,
   Set us, believing, free.

Meet for Thy realm in heaven
   Make us, O holy King!
That through the ages it be given
   To us Thy praise to sing.

The following hymn, in many parts, so much resembles the "Te Deum," that it seems more appropriate to translate it without metre:—

HYMN TO CHRIST.

Daniel, vol. i. p. 46. xxxvii.

(*Christe, Rex cœli, Domine.*)

1 O Lord Christ, King of heaven, great Saviour of the world, who by the gift of the Cross has absolved us from the penalty of death,

2 We beseech Thee to preserve the gifts which by the catholic law Thou hast given to all nations.

3 Thou art the Eternal Word, proceeding from the Father, very God of very God, the only begotten Son.

4 The whole creation, begun at the decree of the Father, by Thy might perfected, doth acknowledge Thee to be the Lord.

5 All the angels show Thy heavenly glory; the choir of the archangels with divine voices praise Thee.

6 The multitude of the four-and-twenty elders, bearing vials full of odours, suppliant adore Thee.

7 Cherubim and Seraphim, Thrones of the Father's light, beating their six wings, to Thee continually do cry,

8 Holy, holy, holy, Lord God of Sabaoth; heaven and earth are full of Thy glory.

9 Hosanna to the Son of David; blessed art Thou of the Father, O Lord, who comest from the highest in the name of God.

10 Thou, the spotless Lamb, hast given Thyself a victim on the earth, who hast washed the robes of the saints in Thine own blood.

11 The host of blessed martyrs dwelling in heaven, glorious with palms and crowns, follow Thee, the Prince of glory.

12 We pray Thee add us to their number, O Lord. With one voice we acknowledge Thee, and praise Thee with one song.

The following verses are extracted from St. Ambrose's celebrated hymn on the Advent. It is the first of the series of translations here selected from the Ambrosian hymns on the truths commemorated in the various festivals :—

ADVENT HYMN.

Daniel, vol. i. p. 12. x.

ST. AMBROSE.

(*Veni, Redemptor gentium.*)

Redeemer of the nations, come ;
Pure offspring of the Virgin's womb,
Seed of the woman, promised long,
Let ages swell thine advent song.

Once from the Father came He forth,
Home to the Father rose from earth ;
The depths of hell the Saviour trod,
Now seated on the throne of God.

To God the Father equal Word,
Thy mortal vesture on Thee gird ;
The weakness of our flesh at length
Sustaining by Thy changeless strength.

Thy cradle shines the darkness through,
Illuming night with lustre new,
Which never night shall hide again,
But faith in ceaseless light retain.

ON THE EPIPHANY.

Daniel, vol. i. p. 127. CVIII.

AURELIUS PRUDENTIUS CLEMENS.

(*O sola magnarum urbium.*)

Small among cities, Bethlehem,
Yet far in greatness passing them;
He who shall King and Saviour be,
The Infinite, is born in thee.

That radiant star, which hath the sun
In beauty and in light outshone,
Proclaims that God has come to earth
In mortal flesh, of human birth.

The Magi, guided by that star,
Their Eastern offerings bring from far;
Prostrate, with vows, their gifts unfold,
Myrrh, frankincense, and royal gold.

Treasures and perfumes rich they bring,
Meet tributes for the God and King;
Embalming frankincense and myrrh
Foretell the mortal sepulchre.

The two following hymns have a peculiar interest as simple narratives, by which, no doubt, the glad tidings were sung into the hearts of the people, although there is a danger of the simplicity of the original sinking in a translation into the jingle of a nursery ballad :—

ON THE PASSION.

Daniel, vol. i. p. 81. LXXVII.

(*Hymnum dicamus Domino.*)

Come let us sing unto the Lord
   A song of highest praise to God,
Who on the accursed and shameful tree [1]
   Redeem'd us by His blood.

The day was sinking into eve,
   The blessed Lord's betrayal-day,
When impious to the Supper came
   He who would Christ betray.

Jesus at that last Supper then
   Tells the disciples what shall be:
"For one of you betrayeth Me,
   Of you who eat with Me."

Judas, by basest greed seduced,
   Seeks to betray Him with a kiss;
He, as a meek and spotless lamb,
   Denies not Judas this.

Thus for some thirty counted pence,
   The impious bargain Judas made;
And Christ, the harmless, blameless Lord,
   Is to the Jews betray'd.

Pilate, the governor, proclaim'd,
   "Lo, I in Him no fault can find;"
Washing in water then his hands,
   Christ to His foes resign'd.

[1] "Patibulo crucis."

The blinded Jews rejected Him,
   And chose a murderer instead;
Of Christ, "Let Him be crucified,"
   With bitter words they said.

Barabbas then is freed, as bound,
   Guilty, and doom'd to death he lies;
And the world's Life is crucified,
   By whom the dead arise.

EASTER HYMN.

Daniel, vol. i. p. 83. LXXIX.

(*Aurora lucis rutilat.*)

The morning kindles all the sky,
The heavens resound with anthems high,
The earth's exulting songs reply,
Hell wails a great and bitter cry.

For He, the strong and rightful King,
Death's heavy fetters severing,
Treads 'neath His feet the ancient Foe,
Redeems a wretched race from woe.

Vainly with rocks His tomb they barr'd,
While Roman guards kept watch and ward;
Majestic from the spoilèd tomb
In pomp of triumph He is come.

Let the long wail at length give place,
The groanings of a sentenced race;
The shining angels, as they speed,
Proclaim, "The Lord is risen indeed!"

The sad apostles mourn'd their loss,
They mused upon the shameful Cross,

They mourn'd their Master basely slain,
They knew not He must rise again.

The women came to embalm the dead;
To them the angel gently said,
With gracious words, "In Galilee
Your risen Lord ye now may see."

Then hasting on their eager way,
The blessed tidings swift to say,
At once their living Lord they meet,
And stoop to kiss His sacred feet.

When the bereaved disciples heard,
Their hearts with speechless joy were stirr'd;
They also haste to Galilee,
Their Lord's adorèd face to see.

The sun the happy world doth cheer
With Easter joy, serene and clear,
As on the Christ, this day of days,
Enrapt, with mortal eyes, they gaze.

His piercèd hands to them He shows,
Where love's divinest radiance glows;
They with the angel's message speed,
Proclaim, "The Lord is risen indeed!"

O Christ, our King compassionate,
Our hearts possess; on Thee we wait,
That we may render praises due
To Thee the endless ages through.

The next hymn is attributed by Mone to St. Ambrose himself:—

EASTER HYMN.

Daniel, vol. i. p. 49. xxxix.

(*Hic est dies verus Dei.*)

This is the very day of God,
Serene with holy light it came—
In which the stream of sacred blood
Swept o'er the world's wide crime and shame.

Lost souls with faith once more it fill'd,
The darkness from blind eyes dissolved;
Whose load of fear too great to yield,
Seeing the dying thief absolved?

Changing the cross for the reward,
That moment's faith obtains his Lord,
Before the just his spirit flies,
The first-fruits enters Paradise.

The angels ponder, wondering,
They see the body's pain and strife,
They see to Christ the guilty cling,
And reap at once the blessed life.

O admirable Mystery!
The sins of all are laid on Thee;
And Thou, to cleanse the world's deep stain,
As man dost bear the sins of men.

What can be beyond this, sublime!
That grace might meet the guilt of time,
Love doth the bonds of fear undo,
And death restores our life anew.

Death's fatal spear himself doth wound;
With his own fetters he is bound.
Lo! dead the Life of all men lies,
That life anew for all might rise;—

>That since death thus hath pass'd on all,
>The dead might all rise again;
>By his own death-blow death might fall,
>And o'er his unshared fall complain.

The following Easter Hymn, among the most ancient of all, Daniel (Thesaurus, i. 89) suggests may have been sung in the early Church by the newly-baptized catechumens, when, in their white robes, they first drew near to partake of the Lord's Supper. This double symbolism does not lessen the beauty of the scriptural imagery :—

EASTER HYMN.

Daniel, vol. i. p. 88. LXXXI.

(*Ad cœnam Agni providi.*)

>The Supper of the Lamb to share,
>We come in vesture white and fair;
>The Red Sea cross'd, our hymn we sing
>To Christ, our Captain and our King.

>His holy body on the cross,
>Parch'd, on that altar hung for us;
>And drinking of His crimson blood,
>We live upon the living God.

>Protected in the Paschal night
>From the destroying angel's might,
>And by a powerful hand set free
>From Pharaoh's bitter slavery.

>For Christ our Passover is slain,
>The Lamb is offer'd not in vain;
>With truth's sincere unleaven'd bread
>His flesh He gave, His blood He shed.

O Victim, worthy Thou for ever,
Who didst the bands of hell dissever,
Redeem Thy captives from the foe,
The gift of life afresh bestow.

When Christ from out the tomb arose,
Victor o'er hell and all His foes,
The tyrant forth in chains He drew,
And planted Paradise anew.

Author of all, to Thee we pray,
In this our Easter-joy to-day;
From every weapon death can wield
Thy trusting people ever shield.

ON THE ASCENSION OF OUR LORD.

Daniel, vol. i. p. 62. LV.

(*Optatus votis omnium.*)

At length the long'd-for joy is given,
 The sacred day begins to shine,
 When Christ our God, our Hope divine
Ascends the radiant steep of heaven.

Ascending where He used to be,
 The Lord resumes His ancient throne;
 The heavenly realms with joys unknown,
Only-begotten, welcome Thee!

The mighty victory is wrought,
 The prince of this world lieth low;
 The Son to God presenteth now
The human flesh in which He fought.

High o'er the clouds, He comes to reign,
  Gives hopes to those who in Him trust;
  The Paradise which Adam lost,
He opens wide to man again.

O mighty joy to all our race!
  The Virgin-born, who bore for us
  The stripes, the spitting, and the cross,
Takes on the Father's throne His place.

To Thee let ceaseless praises rise,
  Champion of our salvation Thou,
  Bearing Thy human body now
In the high palace of the skies.

One common joy this day shall fill
  The hearts of angels and of men;—
  To them that Thou art come again,
To us that Thou art with us still.

Now, following in the steps He trod,
  'Tis ours to look for Christ from heaven,
  And so to live that it be given
To rise with Him at last to God.

ASCENSION HYMN.

Daniel, vol. i. p. 63. LVI.

(*Jesu nostra Redemptio.*)

Jesus, our Redemption now,
Our Desire and Love art Thou;
God before creation's prime,
Man born in the end of time.

What compassion vanquish'd Thee,
Brought Thee to the shameful tree,
Bearing our transgressions there,
Thy redeem'd from death to spare!

Piercing to the depths of hell,
All its strength before Thee fell,
Ransoming Thy captive band,
Seated now at God's right hand.

Love constrain'd Thee, Lord, to this,
That we might partake Thy bliss;
O'er our sin abounds Thy grace—
Satisfy us with Thy face.

Be our joy, we pray Thee, now;
Our reward eternal Thou;
And as countless ages flee,
All our glory be in Thee.

By means of Latin hymns such as these, if all other sacred literature of the period had perished, might we not trace the course of Christian life in the fourth century from hour to hour, and from day to day throughout the year? An ideal life this would indeed be, rather than one led in full by any sinful man on earth. But the ideal is the standard of the actual; the aim shows the direction of the effort, though it may not indeed show how nearly the object was attained.

In the morning, then, these hymns would awake those in whose hearts their melody lived to the shining of an eternal Sun, serene in changeless and life-giving light; and illumined by Him, "spurning sloth, and casting off the works of darkness," they would go forth as children of the Day to the day's work. The third hour reminded them that then Jesus had been crucified; the glow of the southern noon, that then the Light of the world had hung in darkness on the cross for their redemption; at the ninth hour, the cloud had passed from the cross. At evening they lay down in peace, Christ, at once their Light and their Day, shining through the thickest darkness; and in Him they found rest. Midnight also had its radiant cluster of sacred memories; the Paschal Lamb, the praises sung by Paul and Silas in the prison, the cry "The Bridegroom cometh!" Thus the round of sweet and solemn recollections brought them back to the cock-crowing, and they were reminded of that unutterable look with which the Lord turned and looked on Peter, and melted all the ice from his heart. Day after day bore its own story of the creating and redeeming work of God. The manger of the infant Saviour, and the star of Bethlehem, shone through their winter. Spring, with the singing of birds, and the splendour of flowers, and all its visible dawning of new life, brought also the morning of the resurrection; the Easter joy of nature and of the Church burst forth in harmony. Summer led their hearts up through its radiant depths of light to the surpassing glory of the throne where sitteth the ascended Son of God, restored to the right hand of the Father. And with the fulness of life in the natural world came the fulness of life in the spiritual, as Pentecost recalled the descent of the life-giving Spirit to abide with the Church for ever.

These early Latin hymns have in them the healthy upward tendency of early times. They seek rather to pierce the heavens to Christ, than to dive into the heart for emotion. One glorious Person shines above and through them all.

And whilst, from other symptoms, we know that superstition increased, can we not trace in these hymns an advance in the apprehension of the truth? Truth, indeed, came complete to us from God, enshrined in the Incarnate Lord. But is there not in the Church, as well as in the soul, a growth in the knowledge of Christ, a gradual enlightening of the mind to perceive the treasures laid up in Him? The armoury was indeed fully furnished from the first; not one weapon has been added since the Saviour vanquished Satan for us, and St. Paul proved the panoply. But age after age has brought out fresh arms from the inexhaustible store as they were needed. The Arian controversy, whilst it brought forth a quantity of vain subtleties and bitter words, rang from the true metal a sound clearer than it had yielded before. It brought up from the old mine many a jewel for the crown of Him who is King of kings. It struck from the heart of the true Church many an adoring hymn to her Lord.

And in those early Latin hymns is there not a clearer utterance of the great truth of the Cross, the truth which sustains the heart in life and death, than even in the early Oriental hymns? The trust in the Lamb of God, smitten for our transgressions, and bearing our sins, does indeed shine through the Oriental hymns, but is it not more pervading and glowing in the Ambrosian? Is there not, in this respect, more of the impress of the Apostolic Epistles on these last? How frequently the image of the Paschal Lamb recurs in them, the words "redeemed by Thy blood," and the thought of the

Just submitting willingly to the penalty that the unjust might be redeemed, liberated, and made holy! The tone of the "Te Deum" thrills through them all:—"We therefore pray Thee, help Thy servants whom Thou hast redeemed with Thy precious blood;" and it is the echo of a yet earlier and deeper song.

This chapter may be closed by a hymn extracted from a longer poem by Prudentius. It was never incorporated into the public services of the Church until the Reformation, when, after lying comparatively dormant from the fourth century to the sixteenth, it awoke to life as the favourite funeral hymn of the Protestants of Germany. Such it remained for many years, sometimes in the original Latin, and sometimes in a German translation.

FUNERAL HYMN BY PRUDENTIUS.

Daniel, vol. i. p. 137. cv.

(*Jam mœsta quiesce querela.*)

Ah! hush now your mournful complainings,
   Nor, mothers, your sweet babes deplore;
This death we so shrink from but cometh
   The ruin of life to restore.

Who now would the sculptor's rich marble,
   Or beautiful sepulchres, crave?
We lay them but here in their slumber;
   This earth is a couch, not a grave.

This body a desolate casket,
   Deprived of its jewel, we see;
But soon, her old colleague rejoining,
   The soul reunited shall be.

For quickly the day is approaching,
  When life through these cold limbs shall flow;
Through the dwelling, restored to its inmate,
  The old animation shall glow.

The body which lay in dishonour,
  In the mouldering tomb to decay,
Rejoin'd to the spirit which dwelt there,
  Shall soar like a swift bird away.

The seed which we sow in its weakness,
  In the spring shall rise green from the earth;
And the dead we thus mournfully bury,
  In the morning again shall shine forth.

Mother Earth, in thy soft bosom cherish
  Whom we lay to repose in thy dust;
For precious these relics we yield thee:
  Be faithful, O Earth, to thy trust!

This once was the home of a spirit
  Created, and breathed from its God;
The wisdom and love Christ imparteth
  Once held in this frame their abode.

Then shelter the sacred deposit;
  The Maker will claim it of thee;
The Sculptor will never forget it,
  Once form'd in His image to be.

The happy and just times are coming,
  When God every hope shall fulfil;
And visibly then thou must render
  What now in thy keeping lies still.

For though, through the slow lapse of ages,
  These mouldering bones should grow old,
Reduced to a handful of ashes
  A child in its hands might infold;

Though flames should consume it, and breezes
    Invisibly float it away,
Yet the body of man cannot perish,
    Indestructible through its decay.

Yet whilst, O our God, o'er the body
    Thou watchest, to mould it again,
What region of rest hast Thou order'd
    Where the spirit unclothed may remain?

In the bosom of saints is her dwelling,
    Where the fathers and Lazarus are,
Whom the rich man, athirst, in his anguish
    Beholds in their bliss from afar.

We follow Thy words, O Redeemer,
    When, trampling on Death in his pride,
Thou sentest to tread in Thy footsteps
    The thief on the cross at Thy side.

The bright way of Paradise open'd,
    For every believer has space;
And that garden again we may enter
    Which the serpent once closed to our race.

Thus violets sweet, and green branches
    Oft over these relics we strew;
The name on these cold stones engraven
    With perfumes we'll fondly bedew.

It seems well to insert at this point the earliest Vernacular Hymn of any celebrity, the Lorica, or Irish Hymn of St. Patrick, contemporary of St. Ambrose.

ST. PATRICK'S LORICA, OR BREASTPLATE.

I bind to myself to-day
The strong power of the invocation of the Trinity,
The faith of the Trinity in Unity,
The Creator of the Elements.

I bind to myself to-day
The power of the incarnation of Christ with that of His Baptism,
The power of the Crucifixion with that of His Burial,
The power of the Resurrection with the Ascension,
The power of the coming to the Sentence of Judgment.

I bind to myself to-day
The power of the love of Seraphim,
In the obedience of Angels,
In hope of Resurrection unto reward,
In the prayers of the noble Fathers,
In the predictions of the Prophets,
In the preaching of Apostles,
In the faith of Confessors,
In the purity of Holy Virgins,
In the acts of Righteous Men.

I bind to myself to-day
The power of Heaven,
The light of the Sun,
The whiteness of Snow,
The force of Fire,
The flashing of Lightning,
The velocity of Wind,
The depth of the Sea,
The stability of the Earth,
The hardness of Rocks.

I bind to myself to-day
The Power of God to guide me,
The Might of God to uphold me,
The Wisdom of God to teach me,
The Eye of God to watch over me,
The Ear of God to hear me,
The Word of God to give me speech,
The Hand of God to protect me,
The Way of God to prevent me,
The Shield of God to shelter me,
The Host of God to defend me,
    Against the snares of demons,
    Against the temptations of vices,
    Against the lusts of nature,
    Against every man who meditates injury to me,
    Whether far or near,
    With few or with many.

I have set around me all these powers,
Against every hostile savage power
Directed against my body and my soul,
Against the incantations of false prophets,
Against the black laws of heathenism,
Against the false laws of heresy,
Against the deceits of idolatry,
Against the spells of women and smiths and druids,
Against all knowledge which binds the soul of man.

Christ protect me to-day,
Against poison, against burning,
Against drowning, against wound
That I may receive abundant reward.

Christ with me, Christ before me,
Christ behind me, Christ within me,
Christ beneath me, Christ above me,

Christ at my right, Christ at my left,
Christ in the fort,
Christ in the Chariot-seat,
Christ in the poop.

Christ in the heart of every man who thinks of me,
Christ in the mouth of every man who speaks to me,
Christ in every eye that sees me,
Christ in every ear that hears me.

I bind to myself to-day
The strong power of an invocation of the Trinity,
The faith of the Trinity in Unity,
The Creator of the Elements.

Domini est salus
Domini est salus
Christi est salus
Salus tua Domine sit semper nobiscum.

CHAPTER VI

GREGORY THE GREAT, VENANTIUS FORTUNATUS, AND THE VENERABLE BEDE

WE are now approaching the Middle Ages; but before Chivalry, and the Crusaders, Gothic architecture, and the Feudal system, and all the various civil and social elements which are 'generally thought characteristic of that period, had taken definite form, we pass through a border land, left waste for the struggles of the ancient and modern races, literature and civilization. This border land has its rich and wild border minstrelsy, and is as fertile in wonders to us as it was barren of rest and comfort to those who lived in it. Mediæval legend takes wings from thence as from the heroic ages of modern Christendom. Its heroes are canonized saints, an army counted and memorialized by tens of thousands. Old Roman names and titles lie strewn about in picturesque confusion amongst new Gothic names and titles; and the Gothic names further increase the perplexity, by being, for the most part, ashamed of their parentage, and trying to look like Latin. Emperors and kings, prefects and dukes, consuls and counts, peers and paladins, caliphs and empresses, Irish monks and Greek rhetoricians, the "demon Minerva" and Saint Rhadegunda, move about amongst each other in these ages with easy familiarity, and it would be difficult to convict the most extravagant legend of anachronism in recording days when anachronisms were the rule.

The disorder and wretchedness of these golden ages of legend was extreme. Thoughtful men believed that these were the last days. They could see no existing elements which could evolve a world from this chaos, and looked for no amelioration, save in the sudden, manifest destruction of the old order, and the creation of a new. Gregory the Great, Bishop of Rome (590), said, in a sermon, "Those saints, on whose graves we stand, had hearts exalted enough to despise the world in its bloom" (to him, also, the golden age lay in the past!); "there was then long life amongst men, continued prosperity, rest, and peace; and yet, whilst the world was still blooming in itself, its charm had already faded from their hearts. But now, lo! the world itself has faded, and yet its charm over our hearts decays not. Everywhere death, everywhere misery, everywhere destruction: we are smitten on all sides—on all sides bitter waters overflow us; and yet, with senses blinded by earthly passion, we love the very bitterness of the world, we pursue the world flying from our embrace, we cling to the world sinking from our grasp; and, not being able to sustain the sinking world, we, cleaving to it as it sinks, sink with it into the deep. Once the world enchained us by its charms; now it is so full of misery that of itself it points us to God." And again, in another sermon: "Everywhere do we see mourning, everywhere do we hear sighs. The cities are destroyed, the castles are ruined, the fields are laid waste, the whole land is desolate; the villages are empty, and scarcely an inhabitant is left in the cities, and even this scanty remnant of the human race is daily exposed to slaughter. The scourge of heavenly justice is not withdrawn, because, even under the scourge, no amendment takes place. We see some carried into captivity, some maimed, others slain." Any history of the period will show us that this is no denunciatory rhetoric. Wild Gothic hosts plundered Lombardy and Gaul. England and all the shores of Europe were invaded and desolated by northern pirates; and ere the northern tide had subsided into settled channels, it was met by another fierce torrent from the south; and between the devastations of Goth and Saracen, the wretched populations of Western Europe, previously crushed by provincial misgovernment, were tossed helplessly to and fro. Nations there were none. Rome had crushed all the old national life beneath the pressure of her imperial institutions, and now these, in their turn, were crumbling into dust.

But amidst all this tumult and ruin lived one indestructible life, the life of believing Christian men, in and from Christ, the life hidden with Christ in God, but beaming forth, in those dark ages, in countless works of mercy, order, and freedom, found nowhere beside. This central life vibrated even to the utmost circumference of the external Church; ever, indeed, in fainter eddies, as the centre was farther off, yet still, even at the farthest edge to which its influence thrilled, different from anything else in the world. In the days of Ambrose, it gave a freedom which made men free to rebuke the crimes, and resist the unjust exactions, of imperial despotism. In the time of universal tumult and disorder which succeeded, it was the only principle which had power to preserve its own institutions, amidst the inward decay or outward destruction of every institution besides. A high and true manifestation of Christian life also was the steady contest carried on by the Church against slavery; not, it seems, so much from a conscious opposition as from an unconscious, instinctive repulsion. Frequently, also, from the Lives of Saints of those times, we find them impoverishing themselves, straining every means of influence, and even selling Church plate and property, to purchase the redemption of the many captives made in those days of perpetual warfare.

Our work, however, at present, is with the manifestations of Christian life in hymns, rather than in alms; and among the names of the hymn writers of these periods are those of Gregory the Great, Venantius Fortunatus, Bishop of Poictiers, and the Venerable Bede.

M. Guizot, in his "Civilization in Europe," mentions also, amongst the sacred poets of the sixth and seventh centuries, Avitus, Bishop of Vienne; but he seems to have been rather a religious poet than a hymn writer—rather a writer of long poems on scriptural subjects, than one of those whose hymns flowed on into the one great song of the Church, and were carried on the sacred stream from age to age. Were we in search of sacred poetry rather than of hymns, we might probably find more of this in the sermons than in the professedly poetical literature of this period; at least, we might be tempted to this conclusion by comparing the following extract from an Easter sermon of Cæsarius of Arles, with extracts from the sacred poems of Avitus:—

"Behold," he says, "you have heard what of His own good will our Redeemer has accomplished, the Lord of vengeance. When, like a conqueror resplendent and terrible, He reached the land of darkness, the impious legions of hell, affrighted and trembling, began to question one another, saying, 'Who is this terrible one shining white as snow? Never has our Tartarus seen His like; never has the world cast into our abysses any resembling Him. He is an invader, not a debtor; He exacts, but demands not; we see a Judge, not a suppliant; He comes to command, not to yield; to rescue, not to remain. Were our porters slumbering when this Conqueror attacked our gates? If He were a sinner, He were not so mighty; if any fault sullied Him, He would not thus illumine our darkness. If He is God, why is He come? If He is man, how has He ventured? If He is God, what does He in the sepulchre? If He is man, how can He deliver sinners? Whence comes He, so glorious, so strong, so dazzling, so terrible?

Who is He breaking thus boldly through our frontiers, not only not fearing our torments, but delivering others from our chains? Can this be He of whom our prince so lately said, that by His death we should receive the empire of the universe? But if this be He, the hopes of our prince are frustrated; when he thought to conquer, he has been conquered and dethroned. O our prince! what hast thou done, what hast thou designed to do? Behold, this One, by His lustre, has scattered thy darkness, broken thy dungeons, burst thy chains, delivered thy captives, and changed their mourning into joy.'"

Cæsarius speaks elsewhere of selfishness as the root of evil, and love as the root of all good. But it is expressly with hymns, rather than with religious poetry, that we are now concerned; with those lyrical bursts of song which mark the flow of the great tide of Christian life, rather than with those elaborate compositions which prove only the thought and power of an individual mind. The feature which M. Guizot considers characteristic of the whole literature of the sixth and seventh centuries, is characteristic of hymn literature in all ages. "The character of the literature of this period," he writes, "was, that it ceased to be a literature; it had become an action, a power; it sought to act on the depths of the soul, to produce real effects, genuine reformations, effectual conversions. It was not so much a sacred eloquence as a spiritual power."

The hymn of this period most generally familiar to us is the "Veni, Creator Spiritus," which has been frequently attributed to Charlemagne, but which Mone[1] believes to have been the composition of Gregory the Great, Bishop of Rome, A.D. 590. An extract has already been given from one of Gregory's sermons, showing how deeply he was affected by the miseries of his times. He was no isolated monk, no solitary ascetic, occupied merely with the salvation of his own soul from punishment; still less was he a mere religious idler, playing at turning the mysteries of the faith into ingenious rhymes. He was a man who had borne many toils and many honours in the world, had tried the tranquillity of a monastery, and who at last ended his life amidst the manifold avocations of the bishopric of Rome, an office which then professed to combine the labours of a Christian minister with those of a civil governor. His life may therefore be regarded as no especial mountaintop of peculiar sanctity, but as a healthy specimen of the Christian life of his times, and, in connection with brief sketches of the lives of the Venerable Bede, and Fortunatus, Bishop of Poictiers, may give us some characteristic outline of the religious history of the sixth and seventh centuries.

Neander speaks of Gregory the Great as the last of the classical Doctors of the Church; as forming a point of transition between the old Roman civilization and the new Teutonic literature and civilization, which were to characterize the Middle Ages. He seems also to be in some measure a link between the East and the West, standing as he did in connection with many Eastern Bishops,

[1] "Hymni Latini Medii Ævi."

although himself ignorant of the Greek language. Christendom was not yet violently severed into two separate bodies.

His early training was not ecclesiastical, although his first religious impressions appear to have been early received. He was, like Ambrose, of a patrician Roman family; and after distinguishing himself in the studies then considered befitting his rank, being versed in the Latin classics, which were his national literature, and skilled in rhetoric, he was appointed by the Emperor, Justin the younger, prætor of Rome. He held this office, diligently discharging its duties, until he had reached the age of forty. Then, possessed of a fortune looked on as unlimited, and with every avenue to political distinction open to him, he abandoned all, and retired into a monastery. His character does not seem to have been in the slightest degree capricious or weak. It must have been the energy of a nobler ambition, rather than any mere weariness of the world, which led him into this new path. His asceticism, though severe, seems to have been no exaggerated Oriental enthusiasm, but an austere self-restraint; and in becoming a monk, he does not appear to have fled from the active to the contemplative life, but rather to have entered into a higher sphere of activity. At least, whatever may have been his intentions in thus retiring from the world, his character made the monastic life such to him. He founded six monasteries—one in his father's palace at Rome; and of one of these he became abbot.

At the death of the bishop or Pope, Pelagius,

the people took Gregory by force to make him pontiff. These forcible ordinations are so frequent in the lives of canonized saints that they seem to be merely a part of the ordinary ceremonial on such occasions. Gregory's character must have been too genuine for affectation, and appears to have been too strong for morbid scruples. At all events, once on the episcopal throne, it must have seemed to him his natural place, and he acted as if he felt so. The episcopate was to him no mere place of precedence in a ceremonial. Goethe has said, "Happy the people, when the government is a burden rather than a decoration to the ruler!" and to Gregory the episcopal See of Rome was certainly a serious burden, although one under which the strong man marched boldly forward. He seriously considered himself in some sense the responsible head of Christendom; and with that view, whilst he firmly resisted the claim of the Patriarch of Constantinople to the title of "universal bishop," and rejected the same title for himself, he called himself servant of the servants of God, and lived as such. Of his revenues he kept the strictest account. These accounts were preserved for three hundred years in the Vatican. He inspected the minutest details when necessary, and administered all as a just steward for the Church and the poor. The economy of charity was not then studied as it is now, and perhaps Gregory's alms, whilst relieving much real distress, created some idle mendicancy; but in those days of Lombard invasions and Frankish devastations, the wisest charity could scarcely extend beyond supplying the wants of the day and repairing the desolations of the past; and this, by maintaining the poor, and ransoming many captives, Gregory faithfully did. Some poor old men once came to him from Ravenna. He asked them how they had been helped on their journey; and finding that aid had been refused them by Marinian, the new Bishop of Ravenna, once a monk in the same monastery with himself, he wrote to a friend to admonish him thus:—" I am surprised that one who has clothes, who has silver, who has a cellar, should have nothing to give to the poor. Tell him that with his position he must also change his way of life. Let him not think that reading and prayer are enough for him now, nor that he should sit solitary in a corner without bringing forth fruit in action. He must help those who suffer need, and regard the wants of strangers as his own; otherwise, the title of bishop is for him an empty name." These words, with the following, may give some idea of his own labours:—" I must care," he writes, " at once for the bishops and the clergy, the monasteries and the churches; must be vigilant against the snares of enemies, and ever on my guard against the treachery and wickedness of those in authority." His correspondence extended from Alexandria to England, including a Lombard queen, an Eastern emperor and patriarch, and the missionary Augustine. His objects were practical; petitioning for the oppressed, resisting unjust claims, exhorting to fervour in evangelizing labours. His alms-giving, conscientious and extensive as it was, must in itself have been a calling; but he believed the love that gave, and not the thing given, to be the true alms. "The man is incomparably more," he wrote, "than the thing;" and love he spoke of as "the root of every virtue, and the bond which binds all graces into one." With him spiritual blessings, either in giving or receiving, far outweighed temporal. He writes, "It is written, 'Let him that heareth say, Come.' Whoever has heard the voice of heavenly love in his heart may speak words of exhortation to his neighbour. He may perhaps have no bread to give to the needy, but there is something greater, which every one who has a tongue can give. For it is more to refresh the soul destined to eternal life by the nourishment of the Word, than to satisfy the mortal body with earthly bread. Thus, my brethren, withhold not from your neighbour the alms of the Word." He himself continued to preach, when the Lombard armies carried their devastations close to the walls of Rome, whilst, as one of the great vassals of the Eastern empire, he did his best to secure the defence of the city.

We all know the beautiful story of his going into the slave market at Rome, and, touched with the beauty of some English slaves there, exclaiming, "If they were Christians, they were not Angles, but angels;" a sacred pity which never left his heart until he sent Augustine, a Roman abbot, and several fellow-labourers as missionaries to England. Nor was he content with mere external conversions. On hearing of the conversion of Reccared, the Visigothic King of Spain, from the Arian to the Catholic faith, he wrote to Leander, Bishop of

Seville, exhorting him to see that the king proved himself, by his works, a true citizen of the eternal kingdom.

He earnestly pressed on all, clergy and laity, the study of the Bible. He said the sacred words should, by continual intercourse, penetrate into our being. "We must receive through the Spirit in reading what, when occasion serves, we must prove in suffering." He himself must have found the Scriptures his counsellor; for he writes: "God does not answer individual minds by special voices, but He has so arranged His Word as to answer all questions thereby. The answer, 'My grace is sufficient for thee,' was given to Paul that it need not be particularly repeated to each one of us. God does not now answer us by angelic ministrations or special prophetic voices, because the Holy Scriptures include all that is necessary to meet individual cases, and are constructed so as to mould the life of later times by the example of the earlier." He believed, also, that the farther Christian men advance in the divine life, the deeper insight do they gain into their own unworthiness. "For every one," he writes, "is revealed to himself when he becomes enlightened by contact with the true light. In learning what holiness is, he learns also what guilt is." His heart and judgment were against persecution; and although, in the case of heretics, he sometimes recommended very strong constraint, he especially and repeatedly defended the Jews against fanatical oppression. It is pleasant to think that the man who could speak and live words like the following is the author of the hymn to the Holy Spirit, preserved alone of all the ancient metrical hymns in our Church services:—

"O what a consummate artist is the Spirit! No sooner does He touch the soul than His touch is itself a teaching; for at one and the same time He enlightens and converts the human heart; it suddenly turns stranger to what it was, and becomes what it was not."

So much of the faith which, united to the Source of life, worketh by love, dwelt in the heart and shone in the life of Gregory the Great, Bishop of Rome; so much of the truth which inspired St. Paul and set St. Augustine free, actuated him.

The work of his with which his name is most frequently associated, if we except the mission of Augustine to Canterbury, is the improvement or introduction of the Church music known as Gregorian. He improved the choral music transplanted by St. Ambrose from the Eastern into the Western Church, which was founded on the "four authentic modes" of the ancient Greeks— "the Dorian, Phrygian, Lydian, and Mixolydian"— substituting the Octave for the Greek tetrachord, and introducing the Chant known as the Roman Chant, "plain song," or Gregorian tones; so that his name is as closely associated with them as that of St. Ambrose with the psalmody of the Western Church.

Of St. Augustine's writings he was a diligent student, and was, Neander says, "the great means of transmitting the truths they contained to later times."

VENI, CREATOR SPIRITUS.

Daniel, vol. i. p. 213. CLXXXV.

Come, Holy Ghost, our souls inspire,
And lighten with celestial fire.

Thou the anointing Spirit art,
Who dost Thy seven-fold gifts impart.

Thy blessed unction from above,
Is comfort, life, and fire of love.

Enable with perpetual light
The dulness of our blinded sight.

Anoint and cheer our soilèd face
With the abundance of Thy grace.

Keep far our foes, give peace at home :
Where Thou art guide, no ill can come.

Teach us to know the Father, Son,
And Thee, of both, to be but One ;

That, through the ages all along,
This may be our endless song :

> Praise to Thine eternal merit,
> Father, Son, and Holy Spirit !

About the time of the birth of Gregory the Great at Rome, Venantius Fortunatus had reached his twentieth year in the north of Italy. The two men might serve as specimens of the reverse sides of monastic life. Like Gregory, Fortunatus spent his early and middle life among the laity; not, indeed, in laborious civil offices, but in a gay, literary idleness. Among the last of the Latin verse writers, or among the first of the troubadours, he wandered from castle to palace until he paused at the bridal of Sigebert, first King of Austrasia, and wrote his epithalamium. Welcome everywhere, entering into the family festivities of his hosts, and celebrating courtly marriages and festivals, with easy verses, a light, *débonnaire*, kindly nature, liberally endowed with the faculty of enjoying, he seems to have been a child of the South in his capacity for the *dolce far niente* rather than in the stormy passions which often flash and sweep so suddenly over those sunny southern natures. With a heart that could lie still, and find its life in reflecting the life of others, he appears to have passed safely through the temptations of courtly revelries and dangerous intimacies, like a glass mirror, coloured and illuminated by every passing event, and ruffled by none. We only hear of one very close intimacy of his, and that was with Queen Rhadegunda, the wife of Clotaire. This lady was, at the time of this friendship, separated from her husband, and her influence over Fortunatus was so great as entirely to turn at least the outward current of his life. After becoming acquainted with her, he was consecrated a priest, and was made almoner of a monastery at Tours, which she had founded, and where she resided. Not a shadow of scandal has, however, been thrown over this intimacy by French historians, in other cases not remarkable for the charity which thinketh no evil.

Fortunatus seems to have continued the same easy, light-hearted, contented being as before his adopting the religious habit. The twenty-seven poems which he addressed to Saint Rhadegunda and the Abbess Agnes were inspired neither by their beauty nor their virtues, but by their sweetmeats and their fruits. Saint Rhadegunda sends him some milk, and he writes to her, "In the midst of my fasts" (fasts which, from his own account, seem to have been rather medicinal than penitential) "you send me various dishes, and with the sight you put my mind to torture. My eyes contemplate what the physician forbids, and his hand interdicts what my mouth desires. When, however, your goodness gratifies us with this milk, your gifts surpass those of kings. Rejoice, then, I pray, like a good sister, with our pious mother, for at this moment I enjoy the sweet pleasure of being at table."

At the same time, Fortunatus has written three hymns which have taken root in the heart of Christendom, and have been chanted, often doubtless with deep and solemn feeling, during many centuries—the "Vexilla regis prodeunt," the "Pange lingua gloriosi prœlium certaminis," and the "Salve festa dies." These verses are, indeed, not free from a fanciful imagery far removed from the deep and simple earnestness of the Ambrosian hymns. The little elegancies of literary retirement play about them; the silver trappings of legend and fancy make music round them as they go. Compared with those grand old sacred battle-songs, they have too much of the glitter of the tournament on them. Yet, beneath all this, they have a tender and solemn pathos, and, compared with some similar compositions of later times, are simple and true.

Of the outer life of Fortunatus we know nothing, except on its lighter side; of his spiritual life we know nothing, except through his hymns. The intermediate tones are wanting in the picture, and necessarily the effect is jarring. Yet, why should we believe his hymns to be unreal? If all records of the life of Cowper had perished except "John Gilpin," "Lines on the Receipt of a Hamper," and some playful letters to Lady Austin on the one side, and on the other his beautiful hymn,

"God moves in a mysterious way,"

might we not have some difficulty in reconciling the fragments? Yet, we know that Cowper's piety was as genuine as his playfulness.

At all events, the four hymns by Fortunatus which follow have been the channels of the devotions of centuries, and it is chiefly on this account that their translation has been here attempted:—

CRUX BENEDICTA NITET DOMINUS QUA CARNE PEPENDIT.

Daniel, vol. i. p. 168. CXLI.

The blessed Cross shines now to us where once the
    Saviour bled;
Love made Him victim there for us, and there His blood
    was shed.
And with His wounds our wounds He heal'd, and wash'd
    our sins away,
And rescued from the raging wolf the lost and helpless
    prey.

There, with transfixèd palms, He hung, and saved the
    world from loss ; .
And closed the bitter way of death by dying on the Cross!

That Hand was pierced with cruel nails, fix'd till His
    dying breath—
The hand that rescued Paul from crime, and Peter once
    from death !

O mighty in fertility ! O sweet and noble Tree !
What new and precious healing fruit hangs for the world
    on Thee,

Whose fragrance breathes the breath of life into the
    silent dead,—
Gives life to those from whom, long since, earth's pleasant
    light had fled !

No summer heat has power to scorch who in thy shadow
    rest ;
No moonlight chill can harm at night, no burning noon
    molest.

Planted beside the water-flood, unshaken is thy root ;
Thy branch shall never fade, and in all seasons be thy
    fruit :

For round thine arms entwining is the true and living
    Vine,
And from that blood-stain'd stem distils the new and
    heavenly wine !

VEXILLA REGIS PRODEUNT.

Daniel, vol. i. p. 160. CXXXIX.

The Banner of the King goes forth,
    The Cross, the radiant mystery,
Where, in a frame of human birth,
    Man's Maker suffers on the Tree.

Fix'd with the fatal nails to death,
   With outstretch'd hands and piercèd feet
Here the pure Victim yields His breath,
   That our redemption be complete.

And ere had closed that mournful day,
   They wounded with the spear His side:
That He might wash our sins away,
   His blood pour'd forth its crimson tide!

The truth that David learn'd to sing,
   Its deep fulfilment here attains:
"Tell all the earth the Lord is King!"
   Lo! from the Cross, a King He reigns!

O most elect and pleasant Tree,
   Chosen such sacred limbs to bear,
A royal purple clotheth thee;
   The purple of His blood is there!

Blest! on whose arms, in woe sublime,
   The Ransom of the ages lay,
Outweighing all the sins of Time,
   Despoiling Satan of his prey.

A fragrance from thy bark distils
   Surpassing heavenly nectar far;
The noblest fruit thy branches fills,
   Weapon of the victorious war.

Hail altar, Victim hail once more!
   That glorious Passion be adored!
Since death the Life Himself thus bore,
   And by that death our life restored!

There is certainly a great contrast between the view taken in these hymns of the Cross itself, as the instrument of the Passion, and that taken in the earlier hymns and in the New Testament. In the Bible it is called the accursed tree. In the earlier Christian hymns it is more than once spoken of as the *patibulum* [1]—the gallows—and viewed with horror, as the instrument of the humiliation and torture of our Lord. This feeling is surely the deeper, implying a more real comprehension of the cost at which we were redeemed. In later days, when the cross ceased to be known as an instrument of torture, and was regarded only as a sacred symbol, the glory of the victory there won was reflected back on it, and it was honoured as a warrior might honour his sword, or an old Viking his ship, though with a more solemn and reverent emotion, as the weapon of the Great Victory. From this, superstition descended to far lower depths, till the supposed wood of the Cross was worshipped. It is a significant fact that the last two verses of the hymn of Fortunatus here translated, are, in the Roman Breviary, replaced by these words:—"Hail, Cross, only hope in this season of the Passion! give to the pious justice, to the guilty give pardon."

In the following hymn this sentimental honouring of the Cross is carried yet farther than in the two preceding hymns. The second and third verses probably refer to a legend current in the Middle Ages, which ran thus:—When Adam died, Seth obtained from the guardian cherubim of Paradise a branch of the tree from which Eve ate the forbidden fruit. This he planted on Golgotha, called the place of a skull, because Adam was

[1] Translated usually in this volume, "accursed, or shameful tree."

buried there. From this tree, as the ages rolled on, were made the ark of the testimony, the pole on which the brazen serpent was lifted up, and other sacred instruments; and from its wood at length, then growing old and hard, was made the Cross. And thus from the tree of death sprang the tree of life. As an allegory, the story is beautiful, and although the feeling of the following hymn may be less genuine than that of some others, the homage is surely not yet transferred from the Crucified to the Cross. The light which illumines the tree of death still seems to flow from Him who suffered there :—

PANGE LINGUA GLORIOSI PROELIUM CERTAMINIS.

Daniel, vol. i. p. 163. CXL.

Spread, my tongue, the wondrous story of the glorious
    battle far,
What the trophies and the triumphs of the Cross of
    Jesus are,
How the Victim, immolated, vanquish'd in that mighty
    war!

Pitying did the great Redeemer Adam's fall and ruin see,
Sentenced then to death by tasting fruit of the forbidden
    tree.
And he mark'd that wood the weapon of redeeming love
    to be.

Thus the scheme of our redemption was of old in order
    laid,
Thus the wily arts were baffled of the foe who man betray'd.
And the armour of redemption from Death's armoury
    was made.

When the promised sacred fulness of the times at length
  was come,
From the bosom of the Father, from the royal heavenly
  home,
Came to earth the world's Creator, offspring of the
  Virgin's womb!

Laid an infant in the manger, in the stable poor and dim,
Wrapp'd in swaddling-clothes infolding every helpless
  infant limb,
Thus the blessed Virgin Mother mother's care bestow'd
  on Him,

Till the thirty years were finish'd, when the sacrifice
  should be:
Born for this, for this prepared, He gave Himself an
  off'ring free;
On the Cross the Lamb was lifted, immolated on the tree.

Thorns and vinegar and gall, and nails and spear and
  bitter rood,
Thus His sacred limbs were wounded, thus He shed
  that stream of blood,
Earth and ocean, stars and all things, cleansing in its
  precious flood!

Faithful Cross! of all earth's produce only rich and noble
  tree,
No such flower, or leaf, or fruitage, we in all the world
  can see;
Sweet to us thy wood and nails, for sweetest weight is
  hung on thee.

Bend thy branches, lofty Tree, and, yielding, let thine
  arms extend;
Let the rigour of thy nature, soften'd, tenderly unbend,
Since the King of kings Eternal on thine arms they thus
  suspend.

Thou alone wast meet the Ransom of the ages thus to bear,
And for all the shipwreck'd world a port of refuge to prepare,
With that sacred blood anointed of the Lamb shed freely there.

From a poem of Fortunatus, which Daniel calls "most sweet," "in which," he says, "the poet speaks of nature, born again in the spring-time, as welcoming Christ risen from the dead," the following verses were extracted, and have been sung for ten centuries as an Easter hymn:—

SALVE FESTA DIES TOTO VENERABILIS ÆVO.

Daniel, vol. i. p. 169. CXLIII.

Hail, festal day! ever exalted high,
On which God conquer'd hell, and rules the starry sky!
    Hail, festal day! ever exalted high.

See the fresh beauty of the new-born earth,
As with the Lord, His gifts anew come forth,
    Since God hath conquer'd hell, and rules the starry sky.

Christ, after suffering, vanquish'd Satan's powers;
Thus dons the grove its leaves, the grass its flowers;
    Hail, festal day! ever exalted high.

He burst the bands of Hell, through heaven ascending.
Sea, earth, and sky, to God their hymns are sending,
    Since God hath conquer'd hell, and rules the starry sky.

The Crucified reigns God for evermore,
All creatures their Creator now adore;
    Hail, festal day! ever exalted high.

The changing months, the pleasant light of days,
The shining hours the rippling moments praise,
    Since God hath conquer'd hell, and rules the starry sky.

Christ, Maker and Redeemer! Health of all!
Only-begotten Son! on Thee we call!
    Hail, festal day! ever exalted high.

Thou, seeing man sunk in the depths forlorn,
To rescue man, Thyself as man wast born;
    For God hath conquer'd hell, and rules the starry sky.

Author of Life! Death's garments round Thee lay;
To save the lost, Thou treadest Death's dark way;
    Hail, festal day! ever exalted high.

Let Faith to the sure promise lift her eyes;
The third day dawns, Arise, my Buried! rise,
    For God hath conquer'd hell, and rules the starry sky.

From hell's imprison'd shades strike off the chain,
And those who perish from the depths regain.
    Hail, festal day! ever exalted high.

Bring back Thy face, that all its light may see;
Bring back the Day, which died to us with Thee
    Since God hath conquer'd hell, and rules the starry sky.

Countless the hosts Thou savest from the dead,
They follow free where Thou, their Lord, hast led.
    Hail, festal day! ever exalted high.

Taking Thy flesh again, to heaven Thou farest;
Mighty in battle, glorious spoils Thou bearest,
    For God hath conquer'd hell, and rules the starry sky.

These are the four best known hymns of the Italian Venantius Fortunatus, one of the last poets to whom Latin was a mother tongue. After the death of Queen Rhadegunda, he was made Bishop of Poictiers, and died about the close of the sixth century.

The Venerable Bede, the third hymn writer of the period, was far more essentially a monk than either Gregory or Fortunatus. He reflected the brightest side of monastic life, its devout tranquillity and studious retirement. Born at Wearmouth, near Durham, and brought at seven years old to a monastery near his birth-place, all his early associations must have been of the monastery, not of the home. Study his labour, books his world, letters the incidents of his life, from the time when in his youth he removed to the monastery of Jarrow, at the mouth of the Tyne, not an event is recorded as breaking the quiet flow of his days. There, he read, wrote, and prayed, sang hymns to his Saxon harp, and recorded the history of his people, and corresponded with friends in all parts of England and Europe; and there, as the last work of his busy, tranquil life, he translated the Gospel of John into Anglo-Saxon, finishing it amidst the sufferings of his last illness, and dying just as he had concluded the last chapter. He says of himself, "I have used all diligence in the study of the Holy Scriptures, and in the observance of the conventual rules and the daily singing in the church: it was ever my joy either to learn, or to teach, or to write something." His monastic retirement was no idle seclusion: he was at once the historian and the teacher of his times.

England, though vexed with many storms of her own, was in those days little agitated by the tempests which disturbed the Continent. Since the days when Gregory the Great had sent Augustine to Kent, an eager desire for learning had sprung up among the Anglo-Saxons, and many crossed the sea to seek instruction from the Irish monks, who then dwelt apart in an island of peace,—floods of Gothic and Saracen invasion rolling by in the distance. From the East also, from the fatherland of St. Paul, ere the old fountain was quite dried up, a teacher came to England. Theodore of Cilicia was appointed Archbishop of Canterbury, and he made progresses through the country to teach all who would learn. Bede collected these instructions, and treasured them up for his nation. He was surrounded by scholars who revered him and kept by him to the last. From one of these, Cuthbert, Neander (in his "Denkwürdigkeiten des christlichen Lebens") extracts the following account of his deathbed, interesting to us both as a proof of the simplicity of his faith, and as an illustration of the hold the ancient hymns had on the hearts of Christian men of his time. Cuthbert mentions how Bede passed the last weeks of his life, in a sickness which brought him to the grave A. D. 785, in his sixty-third year. The scholar writes: "He lived joyfully, giving thanks to God day and night, yea at all hours, until the Feast of the Ascension; every day he gave lessons to us his pupils, and the rest

of his time he occupied in chanting psalms. He
was awake almost the whole night, and spent it in
joy and thanksgiving; and when he awoke from
his short sleep, immediately he raised his hands on
high, and began again to give thanks. He sang
the words of the Apostle Paul, 'It is a dreadful
thing to fall into the hands of the living God.'
He sang much besides from the Holy Scriptures,
and also many Anglo-Saxon hymns. He sang
antiphons, according to his and our custom (the
ancient custom which Ambrose had introduced
among the people from the East), and among
others this one: 'O King of Glory, Lord of
power! who this day didst ascend a victor above
all the heavens, leave us not orphaned behind
Thee, but send to us the promised Spirit of the
Father. Hallelujah!' And when he came to the
words 'leave us not orphaned behind Thee,' he
burst into tears. Then in an hour he began to
sing again. We wept with him; sometimes we
read, sometimes we wept, but we could not read
without tears. Often would he thank God for
sending him this sickness, and often would he say,
'God chasteneth the son whom He loveth.' Often,
too, would he repeat these words of St. Ambrose:
'I have not lived so that I should be ashamed to
live amongst you; yet neither do I fear to die, for
we have a good Lord.' Besides the lessons which
he gave us, and his psalm-singing during those
days, he composed two important works, a translation of the Gospel of St. John into our native
tongue, for the use of the Church, and Extracts
from Isidore of Seville; for he said, 'I would not

that my pupils should read what is false, and after my death should labour in vain.' On the Tuesday morning before Ascension-day, his sickness increased, his breathing became difficult, and his feet began to swell. Yet he passed the whole day joyfully, dictating. At times he would say, 'Make haste to learn, for I do not know how long I shall remain with you, or whether my Creator will not soon take me to Himself.' The following night he spent in prayers and thanksgiving. And when Wednesday dawned he desired us diligently to continue writing what we had begun. When this was finished, we carried the relics in procession, as is customary on that day. One of us then said to him, 'Dearest master, we have yet one chapter to translate: will it be grievous to thee if we ask thee any further?' He answered, 'It is quite easy; take the pen and write quickly.' At three o'clock he said to me, 'Run quickly and call the priests of this convent to me, that I may impart to them the gift which God has given me.' Then he begged every one of them to offer masses and to pray for him. They all wept, chiefly for that he said that in this world they should see his face no more. But they rejoiced in that he said, 'I go to my Creator; I have lived long enough; the time of my departure is at hand, for I long to depart and be with Christ.' Thus did he live on till the evening. Then that scholar said to him, 'Dearest master, there is only one thought left to write.' He answered, 'Write quickly.' Soon that scholar replied, 'Now this thought also is written.' He answered, 'Thou hast well said. It is finished.

Raise my head in thy hand, for it will do me good to sit opposite my sanctuary, where I was wont to kneel down to pray, that sitting I may call upon my Father.' So he seated himself on the ground in his cell, and sang the 'Glory to Thee, O God, Father, Son, and Holy Ghost;' and when he had named the Holy Ghost, he breathed his last breath."

Such was the calm of a Christian's death-bed in England eleven hundred years ago.

The longest of the Venerable Bede's hymns is a comparison of the six days of creation with the six ages of the world; the sixth day, in which Adam was created, corresponding to the sixth age, in which "He by whom man was created Himself became man"—when, as Eve was formed out of the side of the sleeping Adam, the bride of Christ also was raised to life through Him who slept in death upon the cross. The seventh age was, Bede believed, to be the age of quietness, when Christ shall command the Sabbath, and keep it with His own; and the eighth age is to be "sublime above all the ages, when the dead of the earth shall arise, and the just shall see for ever the face of Christ, and be like the angels on the heavenly heights."

Two other hymns, attributed to Bede by Daniel, may be translated at length.

ON THE ASCENSION OF THE LORD.

Daniel, vol. i. p. 206.   CLXXII.

(*Hymnum canamus gloriæ.*)

A hymn of glory let us sing!
New hymns throughout the world shall ring:
By a new way none ever trod,
Christ mounteth to the throne of God.

The apostles on the mountain stand,
The mystic mount, in Holy Land;
They, with the Virgin-mother, see
Jesus ascend in majesty.

The angels say to the eleven,
"Why stand ye gazing into heaven?
This is the Saviour; this is He!
Jesus hath triumphed gloriously!"

They said the Lord should come again,
As these beheld him rising then,
Calm soaring through the radiant sky,
Mounting its dazzling summits high.

May our affections thither tend,
And thither constantly ascend,
Where, seated on the Father's throne,
Thee reigning in the heavens we own!

Be Thou our present joy, O Lord,
Who wilt be ever our reward;
And as the countless ages flee,
May all our glory be in Thee!

ON THE INNOCENTS.

Daniel, vol. i. p. 207. CLXXVI.

(*Hymnum, canentes martyrum.*)

A hymn of martyrs let us sing!
The innocents remembering,
Of whom, with tears, was earth bereaved,
Whom heaven with songs of joy received;
Whose angels through eternity
The heavenly Father's face shall see,
And to His grace their praises bring:
A hymn of martyrs let us sing!

The following was known to Bede, and as such may have a peculiar interest, besides its general value as showing the way in which the judgment-day was pictured to the Christians of his time:—

ON THE DAY OF JUDGMENT.

Daniel, vol. i. p. 194. CLXI.

(*Apparebit repentina.*)

Suddenly to all appearing the great day of God shall come,
As a thief at darkest midnight on an unsuspecting home:
Brief, indeed, shall all the glory of this age be seen to be,
When the world and all things in it shall have vanish'd visibly.
Then the clangour of the trumpet, sounding clear from depth to height,
All the dead and all the living to Christ's judgment-seat shall cite;

Dazzling in majestic glory shall the Judge from heaven
    descend,
And the radiant hosts of angels worshipping on Him
    attend.
Blood-red then the moon's soft lustre, and the sun grows
    dark on high;
Earth from end to end shall tremble, pale stars falling
    from the sky;
Terrible, before the presence of that justest Judge out-
    pouring,
Flames of fire the earth and heavens and the ocean's
    depths devouring.

On His throne, sublime enthronèd, shall the King of
    Glory sit,
Dreadful hosts of mighty angels terribly surrounding it.
At His right hand then the angels the elect of men shall
    gather;
While the wicked on the left hand, trembling, herd like
    goats together.
"Come, ye blessed," He will say, "and enter on the
    kingdom fair,
By the Father's love preparèd for you, ere the ages were.
Ye who with a brother's kindness succour'd Me, distress'd
    and poor,
Rich with everlasting riches, reap love's guerdon ever-
    more."
The redeem'd with joy exclaiming, ask Him—"When,
    O Christ our King,
Did we see Thee poor and needy, and to Thee our
    succour bring?"
Then that mighty Judge shall answer—"When, in your
    humility,
On the needy home and raiment ye bestow'd, ye gave it
    Me."

Nor will He the bitter sentence of the wicked long delay,
The "Depart from Me, ye cursed, from My presence far away:
Me, imploring aid and pity, have ye scornfully rejected:
Naked, gave to Me no clothing; sick and poor, my woes neglected."
Then the wicked cry, astonished—"When, O great and glorious King,
Did we see Thee sick and needy, and to Thee no succour bring?"
And that mighty Judge shall answer—"When ye, in your luxury,
To the poor refused your aid and pity, ye refused it Me."
Backward, then, the wicked rushing, plunge into the quenchless fire,
Where the worm shall never perish, nor the raging flames expire;
Where the dark infernal prison Satan with his slaves is keeping,
Where they gnash their teeth in anguish, where are ceaseless groans and weeping.
But the faithful to the heavenly country are upborne on high,
'Mid the band of happy angels in the kingdom of the sky;
To Jerusalem Celestial blessed citizens they come,
"Vision" true "of peace" unfading, and their bright unchanging home,
Where the multitudes unnumber'd gaze on Christ the King divine,
See Him with the Father's glory evermore resplendent shine.

Wherefore all the wiles and malice of the ancient serpent
    flee.
Gold and luxury and weakness, if ye in that home would
    be,
Be with purity engirded, as a radiant zone complete,
Let your lamps be brightly shining, and go forth the
    King to meet.

CHAPTER VII

ST. BERNARD

NEVER was there a biography which more fully mirrored the history of the age to which it belongs, and at the same time more truly reflected the light common to all ages and all hearts, than that of Bernard of Clairvaux. The local and the sky colour are wonderfully blended in it. It is at once essentially mediæval and deeply human: it is the one because it is the other. Bernard was no contemplative philosopher enthroned on high above the perplexities and conflicts, the sympathies and errors of his time. He was a man mingling freely with his fellow-men; not beckoning them up to him, but leading them on with him, and pressing on with them; often, indeed, sharing their mistakes, but oftener drawing them onward and upward with himself by the common attraction of that adored Saviour and Son of man, whose character and whose redeeming love were so deeply engraven on his own heart.

He was born A.D. 1091, at Fontaines, near Dijon,

of a knightly family. His early training was received, not from monks, but from his mother, the Lady Aletta; and its influence seems to have remained on him through his life, so that his monastery had much of the nature of a home. His childhood was spent among his father's vineyards and corn-fields in Burgundy, with five brothers and one sister for his playmates, and a mother's eyes watching them all. The six brothers were once more united in after-life under the roof of one monastery.

His mother had consecrated him from the first to God. In his early youth he was sent to the cathedral school of Chatillon-sur-Seine, where he received a learned education, and acquired Latin enough to preach extempore in that language with ease, and to write Latin hymns as heartfelt and unconstrained as if they had been spoken in his own mother tongue.

Aletta had always prayed that Bernard might become a monk. Much of her own life was spent in visiting the poor around her, in succouring the many sufferers by the petty wars of those lawless times, and in ministering to the wants of the clergy. Six months after Bernard's return from the school at Chatillon, the festival of St. Ambrose occurred, on which Aletta had always been accustomed to prepare a feast for the neighbouring clergy. Her health had long been failing, but nevertheless she contrived to make her usual hospitable preparations, and carried on her ordinary avocations until the day arrived. Then she was too weak to leave her bed, but she insisted on the festivities being continued; and when the repast she had prepared but could not share was over, she requested that the "ministers of the Lord" would visit her in her room. They found her strength almost exhausted, and at her request recited in chorus the "Litany of the Dying." She followed them with her failing voice to the words, "By Thy Cross and Passion, Good Lord, deliver us;" and then, signing the cross on her breast, she sank back and ceased to breathe.

Such a death-bed, and such quiet perseverance in loving services to the last, sealed his mother's vows and early teaching on Bernard's heart. And, at last, one day, believing she had appeared to him, he paused on a journey to join his eldest brother (then besieging a neighbouring castle), and entering a road-side church, knelt before the altar, and vowed at once to fulfil his mother's vow.

This, in his own opinion, was the turning-point in his life—his conversion from the world to God. Of that divine object which thenceforward possessed his heart and renewed his whole nature, he himself speaks thus in one of his sermons on the Canticles:[1]—

"From the very beginning of my conversion, my brethren, feeling my own deficiency in virtue, I appropriated to myself this nosegay of myrrh, composed of all the pains and sufferings of my Saviour, of the privations to which He submitted in His childhood, the labours that He endured in His preaching, the fatigue that He underwent in His journeyings, of His watchings in prayer, His

[1] See Neander's "Life of St. Bernard."

temptations in fasting, His tears of compassion, of the snares that were laid for Him in His words, of His perils among false brethren, of the outrages, the spitting, the smiting, the mocking, the insults, the nails—in a word, of all the grief of all kinds that He submitted to for the salvation of man. I have discovered that wisdom consists in meditating on those things, and that in them alone is the perfection of righteousness, the plenitude of knowledge, the riches of salvation, and the abundance of merit. In these contemplations I find relief from sadness, moderation in success, and safety in the royal highway of this life; so that I march on between the good and the evil, scattering on either side the perils by which I am menaced. This is the reason why I have always these things in my mouth, as you know, and always in my heart, as God knoweth: they are habitually occurring in my writings, as every one may see: and my most sublime philosophy is to know Jesus Christ and Him crucified."

With such an ideal before him, " perfect God and perfect man," Bernard could not stoop to any created being as the model of his life or the worship of his heart; and he did not. Mediæval as he was, with an imagination luxuriant to excess, he opposed himself decidedly to the institution of a feast in honour of the immaculate conception of Mary; and said, in reference to it—" We ought not to attribute to Mary that which belongs to one Being alone, to Him who can make all holy, and being Himself free from sin, can purify others from it. Besides Him, all who have descended from Adam must say of themselves that which one of them says in the name of all, 'In sin did my mother conceive me.'" He did, indeed, believe Mary to have been preserved by grace from all sin; but the interval between such an opinion and the assertion of her absolute sinlessness seemed to him wide.

Having chosen to be a monk, Bernard, by the necessity of his ardent nature, chose also the strictest of the monastic orders, and became at first ascetic to the utmost limits of human endurance. He afterwards regretted the bodily infirmities which these austerities had brought on him, and warned others against them. But Bernard's was the kind of character which learns by trying rather than by copying.

After spending some time in the severest convent of his age, that of Stephen Harding, at Citeaux, at the age of twenty-five Bernard was chosen leader of twelve monks who were sent forth to found a new monastery.

The site of this new Abbey was, when they reached it, called the Valley of Wormwood, surrounded by pathless forests, untilled, uncleared, a haunt of banditti; and it was not until after many months of hard manual labour that Bernard and his monks wrung even their daily bread from the stony soil, or contrived any shelter for themselves from the weather. During their work, they were silent, or sang hymns in chorus; and, as they thus toiled and praised God, many who passed by felt the solemn influence of their devotions and industry; the new Abbey rose to the sound of sacred song, and in time the Valley of Wormwood was transformed into the bright Valley of Clairvaux. This was henceforth Bernard's home, and here, as in the father's house of their childhood, his five brothers, and at length his aged father, were again united under one roof.

Many of the fine old forest trees still remained, and Bernard said that the beeches and oaks were often his teachers, and that he had frequently learned more from trees and rocks than from books. His favourite oratory was a quiet bower, twined with flowers, in a recess of the valley; and there perhaps he wrote, and certainly he sang in his heart, his hymns to Christ. His asceticism did not at all events make him forget that nature was the handiwork of his Father, and her voices broken yet true echoes of His. Clairvaux and that woodland oratory were, however, only resting-places in the pauses of a most busy life. He moved freely about in the world, and when he retreated to his Abbey the men and women he had helped and counselled followed him thither, in person, or with letters, and made his retirement only the centre of fresh labours. It is well known how fervently he preached the crusade, and how all Europe was stirred by his appeals; how assembled multitudes throbbed with a common impulse as that emaciated frame and those "dovelike" yet flashing eyes silently enforced the pleadings of that eloquent voice; how kings and burghers, peaceful men and blood-stained warriors, peasant and noble, the criminal and the devout, wept together, and took on them the badge of the Cross. But perhaps it is not so well known how

Bernard looked on this pilgrimage chiefly as the means of spiritual awakening, and valued even the recovery of the sepulchre from the Infidel little in comparison with the recovery of souls from Satan. When he had aroused any, by means of these appeals, to the deeper enthusiasm of the true spiritual crusade to be carried on at home, he deemed the work far higher. Strongly does it testify to his Christlike character, that when a fanatical monk endeavoured to turn the crusading enthusiasm against the Jews, Bernard threw his whole heart into endeavours to check the ferocities which ensued, and did not rest until he had not only calmed the rage of the populace and stopped the persecution, but convinced the instigator of it of his error and sin.

Constantly he acted as a mediator between the oppressor and the oppressed. In every movement and controversy of the age his active nature shared; it can scarcely be hoped, always on the right side. He was against Arnold of Brescia, Henri, the disciple of Peter de Bruys, and all reformers who stood in opposition to the Church, much, it would seem, as Luther was against the Anabaptists of his time; and yet in many ways their best objects were the same. Both desired a real spiritual reformation of the Church, and if Bernard hoped too much from the ecclesiastical institutions of his age, perhaps, on the other hand, his opponents were driven into denying institutions appointed by Christ Himself.

His ideal of the Papacy was very lofty and spiritual. He would have had secular cares and dignities transferred to secular hands, and would have made the Papal throne a judgment seat, not between one covetous man and another ("Who made me a ruler or a judge over you?" he quotes with reference to this), but between the oppressor and the oppressed, a fountain of truth, a seat of righteous judgment, where, as at the bar of God, men should be known not as noble or royal, rich or poor, but as men. None felt the contradiction between the actual and the ideal in this instance more strongly than Bernard himself. But he was not a man to defer his work until his tools were perfect. The time was short, and the work was great; thus he worked on with such instruments as he had, and we must not wonder if the result sometimes shows traces of the imperfect tools.

It is strange to see how almost all religious strifes and theological controversies revolve around two or three points, and are as much alike from age to age as the human frame is beneath its countless varieties of local or historical costume. What a day that will be when all the combatants for existing forms against innovations, and for spiritual truth against forms (all, that is, who loved their Master more than their opinions), shall be reconciled at His feet, and find all the work which they unconsciously united in doing for Him recognized, and all the work they unconsciously did in opposition to each other for the spirit of lies and malice forgiven!

Bernard had also a serious theological contest with Abelard, which ended in the excommunication of Abelard. The extracts given from it in

Neander's "Church History" might almost seem to be taken from popular books of our own time. It was on the nature of the atonement, in relation to the love and justice of God. Without entering into it, the following passages may be quoted from St. Bernard, to show how far (with the deepest conviction that Jesus died for us, and that "His blood cleanseth from all sin,") he was from regarding God as an avenging Judge instead of a loving Father. In answer to the question thrown out by Abelard, whether God could not have redeemed men by His simple will, he replies: "We cannot fathom the sacrament of the Divine will. Yet we can feel the effect of the work; we can be sensible of the benefit. Why did He accomplish that by His blood which He might have accomplished by a word? Ask Himself. It is vouchsafed me to know that the *fact* is so, but not the *wherefore*." In allusion to the scruple which Abelard expressed about admitting that God required the blood of an innocent person, Bernard answers: "It was not the *death* of Christ in itself, but the will of Him who freely offered Himself that was acceptable to God; and because this precious death, procuring the downfall of sin, could only be brought about by sin, so God had no pleasure in the sin, but used it for good. God did not require the death of His Son, but accepted it when offered; He did not thirst for man's blood, but for man's salvation." He concludes with this remark: "Three things here meet together: the humility of self-renunciation; the manifestation of love, even to the death of the cross; the mystery of redemption, whereby He overcame death. The two former parts are nothing without the third. The examples of humility and love are something great, but have no firm foundation without the redemption." [1] These words may serve to throw a deeper light on his hymns to Christ on the Cross.

Bernard was not a mere philanthropist; his friendships were close and deep, and the love entertained for him in return was very strong. His first converts were among his kindred. He commenced his life of seclusion with a society of thirty personal friends. His family circle was formed again in the cloister, and his father died in his arms. Every day he explained the Bible to his monks. Many were his letters of faithful counsel, and everywhere his pathway was thronged with friends. The Abbé Suger, prime minister of France, and one of the acutest statesmen of his day, aroused to thought by his writings, reformed his Abbey, and on his deathbed called Bernard's letters "bread of consolation," and longed only to see his face once more, and then to die. Guillaume, abbot of St. Thierry, was so fascinated with the sweetness and vivacity of his discourse, that, "could he have chosen his lot among all the world had to offer, he would have desired nothing else than to remain always with the man of God, as his servitor." Peter the Venerable, abbot of the rival monastery of Clugny, declared that he "had rather pass his life with Bernard than enjoy all the kingdoms of the world;" and Hildebert, archbishop of Trèves, journeyed to Rome to entreat the Pope to relieve him from his charge, that he

[1] Neander's "Church History," vol. viii. (Bohn's edition.)

might spend the rest of his days at Clairvaux. Constantly we hear of his "angelic countenance," his "dove-like eyes," of the gracious kindness of his manner, and of the "benevolent smile" which habitually lit up his attenuated countenance. His monks loved him as their father, and years of separation, and the dignity of the papal crown, which one of them (Eugenius) attained, could not weaken the tie. Surely to have been so much loved, he must have loved much.

But his dearest and closest friendship was with his brother Gerard. His love for his brother was almost motherly. Gerard at length became seriously ill. During his illness, the abbot wept, and watched, and supplicated his restoration. But Gerard died. Bernard folded up his grief in resolute resignation, and saw his brother buried without a tear. The monks wondered at his firmness, for hitherto, at the death of any of the brotherhood, his heart had overflowed in sorrow. He ascended the pulpit as usual, and, repeating the text, endeavoured calmly to continue his exposition of the Canticles; but old recollections rushed on his heart, and overpowered him. His voice was lost in sobs, and for some minutes he was unable to proceed. Then, recovering himself a little, and feeling the hopelessness of further restraint at that moment, he poured out his grief before "his children," and, in the most touching words, entreated their sympathy.

"Who," he said, "could ever have loved me as he did? He was a brother by blood, but far more by religion. . . . . Thou art in the eternal presence of the Lord Jesus, and hast angels for thy companions; but what have I to fill up the void thou hast left? Fain would I know thy feelings towards me, my brother, my beloved; if, indeed, it is permitted, to one bathing in the floods of Divine radiance, to call to mind our misery, to be occupied with our grief. Yet God is love, and the more closely a soul is united to God the more does it abound in love. . . . . His nature is to have mercy, and to forgive. So, then, thou must needs be merciful, since thou art joined to Him who showeth mercy; and thine affection, though transformed, is no whit diminished. Thou hast laid aside thine infirmities, but not thy love, for 'love abideth;' and throughout eternity thou wilt not forget me. . . . . He hath given, He hath taken away, and while we deplore the loss of Gerard, let us not forget that he was given. God grant, Gerard, I may not have lost thee, but that thou hast preceded me, and I may be with thee where thou art. For of a surety thou hast rejoined those whom in thy last night below thou didst invite to praise God, when suddenly, to the great surprise of all, thou, with a serene countenance and a cheerful voice, didst commence chanting, 'Praise ye the Lord from the heavens; praise Him, all ye angels.' At that moment, O my brother, the day dawned on thee, though it was night to us; the night to thee was all brightness. . . . . Just as I reached his side, I heard him utter aloud those words of Christ, 'Father, into Thy hands I commend my spirit.' Then, repeating the verse over again, and resting on the word 'Father,' 'Father,' he turned to me, and, smiling, said, 'Oh, how gracious of God to be the Father of men; and what an honour for men to be His children;' and then, very distinctly, 'If children, then heirs.' And so he died, and so dying he well-nigh changed my grief into rejoicing, so completely did the sight of his happiness overpower the recollection of my own misery. . . . . O Lord, Thou hast but called for Thine own. Thou hast but taken what belonged to Thee. And now my tears put an end to my words. I pray Thee, teach me to put an end to my tears."

Thus does the loving and the believing heart soar above doubt straight to the feet of the risen Saviour, and there sees the beloved in the presence of Love, blessed for evermore.[1]

At length the excesses of those early austerities, which he deeply regretted, and the wear and tear of sixty years on an enfeebled frame, began to tell, and it became evident that the voice, never silent when there were any oppressed to plead for or any afflicted to comfort, always ready with faithful counsel, or solemn rebuke, or tender consolation, was to be silenced: the loving soul would never cease its melodies, but its sphere was soon to be changed. One labour of love, however, remained for him to do.

He was reduced to extreme weakness, and confined to his bed, awaiting his release from sin and pain, when he was entreated to mediate in a

[1] Bernard's Abbey was a reformatory as well as a home. He once rescued a criminal on his way to execution by his intercessions, threw his own cowl over him, and brought him back to the discipline of Clairvaux, where, thirty years afterwards, the condemned felon is said to have died a true penitent.

fierce feud between the burghers of Metz and the neighbouring barons, who, in their mutual animosity, were ruining each other and devastating all the country around. Such a call, at any sacrifice, Bernard could not refuse. Perhaps he thought of his mother, with her failing strength, preparing that feast for the festival of St. Ambrose. Perhaps he thought of his Lord sitting weary on the well, yet finding it His meat and drink to fulfil the will of His Father in bringing back one lost sheep to the fold.

Suffering and feeble as he was, he caused himself to be removed to the scene of contest on the banks of the Moselle. The barons had at that time the advantage, and contemptuously rejected his mediation, declaring that they would give battle on the morrow. The night only intervened, doubtless spent by Bernard, like so many by his Master, in prayer to God. In the morning his friends were lamenting the failure of his efforts:—

"Fear not," he said. "I know, from a dream I have had to-night, they will yet yield. I was saying the mass, when I remembered with shame that I had forgotten the angel's song, 'Glory to God in the highest,' and thereupon I commenced and sang it through with you all."

That very afternoon a message did, indeed, arrive from the nobles, announcing that they had changed their determination. In the quiet of the night the recollection of his words of peace had pierced their hearts, and they were ready to listen to terms. Bernard turned joyfully to his friends, and exclaimed, "Behold, here is the introduction to the song, which we shall so soon have to sing, 'Glory to God in the highest, and on earth peace, good will toward men.'"

After a few days of negotiation, in consequence of Bernard's earnest intercessions and patient mediation, a reconciliation was effected, peace was restored, and the peacemaker returned to Clairvaux to die.

His pains grew more intense, his prostration of strength more complete, and even the respite of a few moments' sleep was withheld from him. After alluding to his sufferings in a letter of thanks to a friend who had sent him some fruit, he breaks off abruptly, adding, "I speak as a fool; the spirit is willing, though the flesh is weak."

His last strength was spent in supplicating his monks, in the words of St. Paul, "to abound more and more in every good work;" and as their grief could no longer be restrained, and they stood sobbing around his bed, his eyes filled with tears, and he murmured—"I am in a strait betwixt two, having a desire to depart and be with Christ, which is far better; nevertheless the love of my children urgeth me to remain here below."

These were his last words. Then, fixing his "dovelike eyes on heaven," his spirit passed away from earth, to be, where Gerard and his mother were, "for ever with the Lord." He died at the age of sixty-two, in the year 1153.

His inner life may be farther traced in the three translations of his hymns which close this chapter. This sketch of his history has been given more in detail, because the biographies of the other mediæval hymn-writers contain little more than the date of their existence, and the names of their monasteries and of their writings, and because his life was so illustrative of the Christian life of his times, and so bound up with its history. Many waifs and strays of mediæval hymn literature have been incorrectly assigned to him as a kind of lord of the manor; but those here translated seem admitted, after strict investigation, to be his.

The first is a selection from a series of hymns, inspired by a contemplation of the wounds of the Saviour on the Cross. It has suggested one of Paul Gerhard's most beautiful hymns, though Gerhard's hymn is too original and free to be called a translation. The hymn found in our Moravian and Wesleyan hymn-books, beginning "O head, so full of bruises," is a translation of Gerhard's, and so a lineal descendant of the verses of St. Bernard, of which the following lines are intended to be a translation :—

HYMN TO CHRIST ON THE CROSS.

Trench, "Sacred Latin Poetry," p. 139.

(*Salve Caput cruentatum.*)

Hail, thou Head! so bruised and wounded,
With the crown of thorns surrounded,
Smitten with the mocking reed,
Wounds which may not cease to bleed
    Trickling faint and slow.

Hail! from whose most blessed brow
None can wipe the blood-drops now;

All the bloom of life has fled,
Mortal paleness there instead ;
Thou before whose presence dread
    Angels trembling bow.

All Thy vigour and Thy life
Fading in this bitter strife ;
Death his stamp on Thee has set
Hollow and emaciate,
    Faint and drooping there.
Thou this agony and scorn
Hast for me, a sinner, borne,
Me, unworthy, all for me !
With those signs of love on Thee,
    Glorious Face, appear !

Yet in this Thine agony,
Faithful Shepherd, think of me ;
From whose lips of love divine
Sweetest draughts of life are mine,
    Purest honey flows.
All unworthy of Thy thought,
Guilty, yet reject me not ;
Unto me Thy head incline,
Let that dying head of Thine
    In mine arms repose !

Let me true communion know
With Thee in Thy sacred woe,
Counting all beside but dross,
Dying with Thee on Thy Cross ;—
    'Neath it will I die !
Thanks to Thee with ev'ry breath,
Jesus, for Thy bitter death ;
Grant Thy guilty one this prayer,
When my dying hour is near,
    Gracious God, be nigh !

When my dying hour must be,
Be not absent then from me;
In that dreadful hour, I pray,
Jesus, come without delay.
    See and set me free!
When Thou biddest me depart,
Whom I cleave to with my heart,
Lover of my soul! be near,
With Thy saving Cross appear,
    Show Thyself to me!

It is interesting to think that this prayer for his last hours was written by one who had been present when Aletta had sunk back and died with so similar a petition on her lips, and had witnessed the calm which the presence of that crucified Saviour had shed on the death-bed of Gerhard.

The next is from that portion of the same hymn devoted to the contemplation of the pierced feet of the Saviour :—

SALVE MUNDI SALUTARE.

Trench, p. 137.

All the world's salvation, hail!
Jesus, Saviour, hail, oh hail!
I would be conformèd now
To Thy Cross; Thou knowest how!
    Grant Thy strength to me!
And, if present, oh, receive me!
Ever present I believe Thee,
Pure and spotless, I adore Thee,
See me, prostrate, here before Thee,
    Be Thy pardon free.

Wounded feet, with nails pierced through,
Fix'd till death those bonds undo,
Tenderly I thus embrace,
Gazing, trembling, on Thy face,
   On Thy love so endless.
Wounded, we Thy healing prove,
Thank Thee for Thy matchless love;
Friend of sinners, suffering there,
Thou our ruin canst repair,
   Father of the friendless!

What in me is maim'd and shatter'd,
Misapplied, or vainly scatter'd,
Oh, sweet Jesus! heal again;
Make my heart's rough places plain,
   By Thy healing rood.
Thee upon Thy cross I seek,
Helpless is my soul, and weak!
Thou wilt cure as I have craved,
Heal me, and I shall be saved,
   Wash me in Thy blood.

Fix, oh, fix each crimson wound,
And those nail-prints so profound;
In my heart engrave them fully,
That I may grow like Thee wholly,
   Jesus, Saviour sweet!
Pitying God, to Thee I cry;
Guilty at Thy feet I lie:
Oh, be merciful to me,
Nor bid me, unworthy, flee
   From Thy sacred feet!

Prostrate, see, Thy Cross I grasp,
And thy piercèd feet I clasp;

Gracious Jesus, spurn me not;
On me, with compassion fraught,
    Let Thy glances fall.
From Thy Cross of agony,
My Beloved, look on me;
Turn me wholly unto Thee;
"Be thou whole," say openly,
    "I forgive thee all."

    The other hymn has been translated by Count Zinzendorf, or rather, poured from St. Bernard's heart into his, and then given out, in German, fresh as from a fresh source. The original hymn, from which the following verses are translated, is very long :—

JESU DULCIS MEMORIA.
Trench, p. 246.

O Jesus! Thy sweet memory
Can fill the heart with ecstasy;
But passing all things sweet that be,
    Thine actual presence, Lord!

Never was sung a sweeter word,
Nor fuller music e'er was heard,
Nor deeper aught the heart hath stirr'd,
    Than Jesus, Son of God!

What hope, O Jesus, Thou canst render
To those who other hopes surrender—
To those who seek Thee, oh, how tender,
    But what to those who find!

Jesus, the fragrance of the heart,
The only Fount of Truth Thou art,
Who dost true life and joy impart,
    Surpassing all desire.

No tongue suffices to confess,
No letters can enough express,
The heart that proves believes the bliss,
    What it is Christ to love!

With Mary, ere the morning break,
Him at the sepulchre I seek,
Would hear Him to my spirit speak,
    And see Him with my heart.

O Jesus, King unspeakable!
Victor, whose triumphs none can tell—
Whose goodness is ineffable,
    Alone to be desired:

When Thou dost in our hearts appear,
Truth shines with glorious light, and clear;
The world's joys seem the dross they are,
    And love burns bright within.

Thy love was proved upon the Cross,
The shedding of Thy blood for us,
Our free redemption granting thus,
    And the blest sight of God.

Who taste Thy love, true food obtain;
Who drink, for ever thirst again;
All other joys seem poor and vain
    Beside this passing love.

Jesus, the strength of angels strong,
Thy name excels the sweetest song,
Dropping like honey from the tongue,
    Like nectar in the heart.

Wherever I may chance to be,
Thee first my heart desires to see;
How glad when I discover Thee,
    How blest when I retain!

Beyond all treasures is Thy grace.
Oh, when wilt Thou Thy steps retrace,
And satisfy me with Thy face,
    And make me wholly glad?

Then come, oh come, Thou perfect King,
Of boundless glory, boundless spring;
Arise, and fullest daylight bring,
    Jesus expected long!

Fountain of mercy and of love,
Sun of the Fatherland above,
The cloud of sadness far remove,
    The light of glory give!

From God's right hand, Thy rightful throne,
Return, Beloved, to Thine own;
Thy victory has long been won,
    Oh, claim Thy conquest now!

The heavenly choirs Thy name, Lord, greet,
And evermore Thy praise repeat;
Thou fillest heaven with joy complete,
    Making our peace with God.

Jesus has gone to heaven again,
High on the Father's throne to reign;
My heart no more can here remain,
    But after Him has gone.

We follow Thee with praises there,
With hymn, and vow, and suppliant prayer:
In Thy celestial home to share,
    Grant us, O Lord, with Thee.

CHAPTER VIII

MEDIÆVAL HYMNS

THE biographies of the other mediæval hymn-writers, whose hymns are translated in these pages, are so little known, that we must look on their modes of living and thinking through those of St. Bernard.

With one exception, all were monks, and the monotonous routine of monastic life seems in their histories to have replaced the endless varieties of discipline by which our heavenly Father trains His children. Doubtless, could we penetrate beneath the cowl and within the convent walls, which time has now so firmly sealed, we should see that even there, uniform as the outward life was, the varieties of inward training were as many as the individual souls there trained. Doubtless, whilst these monks rigidly subjected themselves to one arbitrary rule of living, and praying, and abstaining, beneath this rule, and crossing it, God's hand was at work, with his own separate discipline for each character, testing by sickness, proving by disappointment, sustaining by especial promises, stirring each heart by special blessings. But to us their biographies are mostly lost in the history of the Communities to which they belonged. Adam of St. Victor, the author of thirty-six of the most celebrated mediæval hymns, was a contemporary of St. Bernard, and a member of the illustrious religious house of St. Victor at Paris. Thomas of Celano, supposed author of the "Dies Iræ," was an Italian from the Abruzzi who became a Franciscan friar, a devoted friend and biographer of St. Francis. Thomas à Kempis was a Dutchman, born at Overyssel in 1380, of the Order of the Fratres Communis Vitæ. Their minds and hearts are to us only revealed in their writings.

The one exception to the monastic character of mediæval hymn-writers is King Robert the Second of France, author of the touching hymn, in which all his gentle nature seems to speak, "Veni, Sancte Spiritus;" and King Robert had certainly more of the monk than of the king about him. He seems to have been, if ever any man was, made for the cloister, and being forced into the publicity of the throne, he threw as much as possible of the colouring of the convent over his home and his court. Necessity drove him to the cares and the state of royalty; but his joys were in church music, which he composed, in devotion, and in alms-giving. His mind was his hermitage, and in its cloistral quiet he dwelt apart, enclosed by sacred spells of melody and song. King Robert is hardly an exception to the fact that the hymn-writers of the Middle Ages were all devoted to the monastic life. The son of

Hugh Capet, he ascended the throne of France A.D. 987, and died A.D. 1031. His hymn, "Veni, Sancte Spiritus," was therefore probably composed about the commencement of the eleventh century, when the accents of the sacred song were taken up by Peter Damiani, Cardinal Bishop of Ostia, said to have been a zealous reprover of the popular vices and clerical ambition of his time. He died A.D. 1071. His most beautiful hymn is the one on the Joys of Paradise, frequently attributed to St. Augustine.

Twenty years later (about A.D. 1091) St. Bernard was born, and he with his contemporaries, Adam of St. Victor, Hildebert, Peter the Venerable, and Bernard of Clugny, filled the Church with hymns of praise all through the twelfth century. That century, the great era of the Crusades, was the harvest-field of mediæval hymns. Those belonging to an earlier or a later period are comparatively mere first-fruits or after-gleanings. Then it was that the great theological school of St. Victor tried to reconcile the dialectic and the mystic theology, and its poet was Adam of St. Victor, with his elaborate system of scriptural types occasionally chilling the genuine fire of his verse into a catalogue of images. Then Peter the Venerable ruled the Abbey of Clugny with his gentle sceptre; caused the Koran to be translated, that Mohammedanism might be understood and refuted, and the Moslem converted rather than slain; received the excommunicated Abelard to his monastery, watched over him, and finally accomplished a reconciliation between him and St. Bernard. The beatitude of the peace-maker seems to have rested on this venerable man, and the translation of his hymn, "Mortis portis fractis, fortis," may give some idea of his joyful faith in the Resurrection.

After this chorus there is a brief silence, the echoes of that burst of song sounding on through the ages, until they blend with the rising tones of a new psalm, and are lost in the solemn and magnificent chant of the great mediæval hymn, the "Dies Iræ." That hymn rose alone in a comparative pause, as if Christendom had been hushed to listen to its deep music, ranging as it does through so many tones of human feeling, from trembling awe, and the low murmurs of confession, to tender pathetic pleading with One who, though the "just avenging Judge," yet "sate weary" on the well of Samaria, seeking the lost, trod the mournful way, and died the bitterest death for sinful men. Its supposed author, Thomas of Celano, in the Abruzzi, lived during the fourteenth century, was a Franciscan monk, and a personal friend of St. Francis himself whose life he wrote. But so much doubt has hung about the authorship, and if Thomas of Celano was the author, so little is known of him, even the date of his birth and death not being ascertained, that we may perhaps best think of the "Dies Iræ" as a solemn strain sung by an invisible singer.

There is a hush in the great choral service of the universal Church, when suddenly, we scarcely know whence, a single voice, low and trembling, breaks the silence; so low and grave that it seems to deepen the stillness, yet so clear and deep that its softest tones and words are heard throughout

Christendom, and vibrate through every heart; grand and echoing as an organ, yet homely and human, as if the words were spoken rather than sung. And through the listening multitudes solemnly that melody flows on, sung not to the multitudes, but " to the Lord," and therefore carrying with it the hearts of men, till the singer is no more solitary, but the selfsame tearful, solemn strain pours from the lips of the whole Church as if from one voice, and yet each one sings it as if alone to God.

Thomas à Kempis (born 1386, died 1471), supposed author of the " Imitation of Christ," next takes up the strain, and it is interesting, through those lines of his on " The Joys of Heaven," to follow the patient bearer of the cross up to the blessed city, "whose gates" (in the words of another mediæval hymn-writer, Hildebert, Archbishop of Tours) "are the wood of the Cross;" not, indeed, the cross of the disciple, but of the Master.

The latest mediæval hymn-writer, among those whose hymns are translated in these pages, is John Mauburn, Abbot of Livry, who was born at Brussels, and died A.D. 1502. His name may close the list of mediæval singers, whose hymns were emphatically songs in the night.

The following translations are arranged according to their subjects, not according to their authors. This arrangement follows the sacred history of the Gospels and the Acts of the Apostles, as traced in the annual festivals of the Church, embracing the great objects of Christian faith, and concluding with hymns on the joys of heaven, and on more miscellaneous subjects.

The first two are on the Nativity. Both are of late date, were incorporated, with and without translation, into the Protestant German hymn-books, and sung in the Lutheran churches after the Reformation; the old mediæval song thus melting into that of the Reformed Church.

This brief selection from the Latin Hymns of the Middle Ages may well end in the Canticum Solis of St. Francis D'Assisi. Contemporary of Dante, his hymn, like the *Divina Commedia*, is in Italian, thus leading up to the new era of Sacred Poetry in the language of the people.

CHRISTMAS HYMN.

(*Puer natus in Bethlehem.*)

Trench, p. 97.

The Child is born in Bethlehem,
Sing and be glad, Jerusalem!

Low on the manger lieth He,
Whose reign no bound or end can see.

The ox and ass their Owner know,
And own their Lord, thus stooping low.

The kings bring from the farthest East
Gold, frankincense, and myrrh to Christ.

That lowly dwelling entering,
Reverent they greet the new-born King.

Born of a virgin mother mild,
Seed of the woman, wondrous Child!

Born of our blood, without the sin,
The serpent's venom, left therein.

Like us, in flesh of human frame,
Unlike in sin alone He came;

That He might make us sinful men,
Like God, and like Himself again.

In this, our Christmas happiness,
The Lord with festive hymns we bless:

The Holy Trinity be praised,
To God our ceaseless thanks be raised!

HYMN ON THE NATIVITY.

Trench, p. 114.

JOHN MAUBURN—BRUSSELS, 1460–1502.

(*Heu quid jaces stabulo.*)

Dost Thou in a manger lie,
   Who hast all created,
Stretching infant hands on high,
   Saviour long awaited!
If a monarch, where Thy state?
Where Thy court on Thee to wait?
   Royal purple where?
Here no regal pomp we see,
Nought but need and penury;
   Why thus cradled here?

Pitying love for fallen man
   Brought me down thus low,
For a race deep lost in sin,
   Rushing into woe.
By this lowly birth of mine,
Countless riches shall be thine,
   Matchless gifts, and free;
Willingly this yoke I take,
And this sacrifice I make,
   Heaping joys for thee.

Fervent praise would I to Thee
    Evermore be raising;
For Thy wondrous love to me
    Praising, praising, praising.
Glory, glory, be for ever
Unto that most bounteous Giver,
    And that loving Lord!
Better witness to Thy worth,
Purer praise than ours on earth,
    Angels' songs afford.

MEDITATIONS ON THE SUFFERINGS OF OUR LORD.[1]

Trench, p. 134.

ANSELM OF LUCCA—DIED 1086.

(*Desere jam, anima, lectulum soporis.*)

Rise, my soul, from slumber now, leave the bed of sleep;
Languor, torpor, vanity, all outside must keep;
While the heart, lit up within, with love's torches glows,
Dwelling on that wondrous work, and the Saviour's woes.

Reason, thought, affections true, gather all together,
Nor, by trifles led astray, hither roam and thither;
Fancies wild, distracting doubts, busy cares depart,
While the sacraments of life pass before the heart.

Jesu, Sovereign Lord of Heaven, sweetest Friend to me,
King of all the universe, all was made by Thee;
Who can know or comprehend the wonders Thou hast wrought,
Since the saving of the lost Thee so low hast brought?

---

[1] Translated from an extract given in Trench's "Sacred Latin Poetry," from a long poem on the subject.

Thee the love of souls drew down from beyond the sky,
Drew Thee from Thy glorious home, Thy palace bright and high!
To this narrow vale of tears Thou Thy footsteps bendest,
Hard the work Thou tak'st on Thee, rough the way Thou wendest.

The Joy of all is plunged in grief, the Light of all is waning;
The Bread of life needs nourishing, the Strength of all sustaining;
The fount of which all heaven is filled, the Fount of life is thirsting!
What heart such wonders can behold, and not be nigh to bursting?

Oh! faithful Saviour, wonderful Thy gracious condescension,
The depths of Thy most tender love exceed all comprehension;
Spotless art Thou, no sin in Thee, that now Thou thus shouldst languish,
I am the cause, O Jesus, I!—of this Thy bitter anguish.

I exalt myself in pride; Thou art humbled low;
Mine the sins; the penalty, My Saviour, bearest Thou!
I seek soft and easy paths; Thine was hardness all:
Whilst my cup is fill'd with sweets, Thine was mix'd with gall!

The two following hymns on the Cross and Passion have been chosen because they dwell less on the details of bodily anguish than on the love which endured them, and the blessings they won for us; because the Cross is so simply held forth in them as the manifestation of the love of God, and the means of the redemption of man.

Of the first, a Dutch translation (existing in the fifteenth century) is given by Mone. The original Latin may therefore have been of earlier date. These verses are interesting, as having formed an aid to the daily devotions of Christians of that age.

The second of these hymns has been attributed to St. Bernard, but is not in his works, although, Mone says, worthy to be his:—

THE HOURS OF THE PASSION OF OUR LORD JESUS CHRIST.

Mone, "Hymni Latini Medii Ævi," vol. i. p. 87.

AT PRIME.

(*Tu qui velatus facie.*)

O Thou who, though with veilèd face,
Wast still the Sun of righteousness;
With fainting limbs and footsteps slow,
Smitten with many a scornful blow:

With hearts intent we Thee entreat,
Extend to us Thy mercy sweet;
And for Thy loving kindness' sake,
Let us Thy glory all partake.

Honour and praise to Christ be paid,
Once sold and causelessly betray'd;
Who for His people willingly
Bore death upon the shameful tree.

AT TERCE.

(*Horâ qui ductus tertiâ.*)

Thou who at the third hour wast led,
O Christ, to meet that torture dread;

Who on Thy shoulder didst for us,
For us, unhappy, bear the Cross;

Make us so full of love to Thee,
And let our lives so holy be,
That we may win Thy tranquil rest,
And in the heavenly land be blest.

AT SEXT.

(Crucem pro nobis subiit.)

For us the bitter Cross He bore
    And stretch'd thereon was parch'd with thirst,—
    Jesus, whose sacred hands were pierced,
Whose sacred feet with nails they tore.

Honour and blessing we will bring
    To Him, the Lord, the Crucified,
    Who, by His sufferings as He died,
Has ransom'd us from perishing.

AT NONES.

(Beata Christi passio.)

Christ's blessed Passion set us free,
His death our liberation be,
Since endless joys are won by this,
For us eternal heavenly bliss.

Glory to Christ the Lord be sung,
Who, as upon the cross He hung,
With that great cry gave up the ghost,
Saving a world undone and lost.

AT COMPLINE.

(Qui jacuisti mortuus.)

O Thou who layedst dead, the King,
   The spotless King, in peace at last,
   Grant us in peace in Thee to rest,
And evermore Thy praise to sing.

O succour us, our Lord, and bless
   Whom Thou redeemedst with Thy blood;
   And grant us in Thy blest abode
Sweet joys of deep eternal peace.

ON THE PASSION OF OUR LORD.

Mone, vol. i. p. 118.

(Dulcis[1] *Jesu spes pauperum.)*

Jesus! Refuge of the poor
And the wretched evermore;
Wretched unto Thee I flee,
Thirst with all my heart for Thee.
God! whom more than all I prize,
Unto Thee my groans arise;
Thee my weeping voice implores,
Thee my lowly heart adores.

Jesus! nothing is more sweet,
Nothing more with joy replete,
Than to ponder o'er and o'er
All Thy sufferings long and sore;

---

[1] This epithet "dulcis" is omitted, as not precisely rendered by any corresponding English adjective. Three verses have been omitted from this hymn, though simple and touching, as not characteristic of the subject, and therefore, in a translation, tending to weaken the whole.

The memory of Thy death transcending
Sweetest ointments richly blending,
Balsams, spices, rarest scents,
Myrrh, and nard, and frankincense.

Jesus! Lord, what hast Thou done!
Thou no cross by sin hast won!
We deserve what Thou sustainest,
We have earned the cup Thou drainest.
We of Adam's race forlorn,
Thou of a pure Virgin born;
From our birth our sin doth flow,
From Thy birth most pure art Thou.

Jesus! what Thou sufferest there
For the wretched Thou dost bear,
Whom, in the fell tyrant's chains,
Thou didst see 'neath direst pains,
No necessity on Thee
Laid these pains, but mercy free;
Grace made Thee endure the Cross,
Drink the cup of death for us.

Jesus! look upon me here,
Nor despise a sinner's prayer;
Thou all given up to woe,
By Thy hands with nails pierced through,
By Thy side with scourges torn,
By Thy head thus crown'd with thorn,
Spit on, mock'd with many a stroke,
By Thy neck bent 'neath the yoke.

Jesus! Teacher who canst bless!
The holy stream, the dew of grace,
Flowing from Thy wounded side,
Flowing in a crimson tide!

Our remission's ransom price,
Our salvation's sacrifice,
From Thy piercèd hands it flow'd,
From Thy feet nail'd to the rood.

Jesus! once a victim made,
Sold, and to Thy foes betray'd;
By their rage, with envy mix'd,
To the torturing cross affix'd,
Wounded by the spear at last,
'Neath the stone imprison'd fast;
Victor now beyond the sky,
Haste to save us, oh be nigh!

Jesus! merciful Thou art,
Light the sunbeam in my heart,
Thou who, cleansing in Thy blood,
Hast redeem'd me unto God!
To Father, Son, be honour meet,
And to the holy Paraclete;
All honour to the Trinity,
Through ages that no close shall see.

ON THE RESURRECTION OF OUR LORD.

Trench, p. 157.

PETER THE VENERABLE, ABBOT OF CLUGNY—1092-1156.

(*Mortis portis fractis, fortis.*)

Lo, the gates of death are broken,
  And the strong man arm'd is spoil'd
Of his armour, which he trusted,
  By the Stronger Arm despoil'd.
    Vanquish'd is the prince of hell,
    Smitten by the Cross he fell.

Then the purest light resplendent
   Shone those seats of darkness through,
When, to save whom He created,
   God will'd to create anew.

That the sinner might not perish,
   For him the Creator dies,
By Whose death our dark lot changing,
   Life again for us doth rise.

Satan groan'd, defeated then,
   When the Victor ransom'd men ;
Fatal was to him the strife,
   Unto man the source of life ;
     Captured as he seized his prey,
     He is slain as he would slay.

Thus the King all hell hath vanquish'd
   Gloriously and mightily ;
On the first day leaving Hades,
   Victor He returns on high ;

With Himself mankind upraising,
   When He rose from out the grave,
Thus restoring what creating
   In its origin He gave.

By the sufferings of his Maker,
   To his perfect Paradise
To first dweller thus returneth ;
   Wherefore these glad songs arise.

ADAM OF ST. VICTOR—TWELFTH CENTURY.

Trench, p. 159.

(*Pone luctum Magdalena.*)

Lay aside thy mourning, Mary,
   Weep no longer, Magdalen ;

This is not the feast of Simon,[1]
   Tears became thy true heart then.
Thousand causes here of gladness,
Thousand ! and not one of sadness.
     Let thine Alleluia rise !

Clothe thyself in gladness, Mary,
   Let thy brow shine calm and clear ;
All the pain and grief has vanish'd,
   And the glorious Light is here.
Christ hath burst the world's dark prison,
Over death triumphant risen.
     Let thine Alleluia rise !

Lift thy voice rejoicing, Mary,
   Christ hath risen from the tomb ;
Sad the scene He pass'd through lately,
   Now a Victor He is come.
Whom thy tears in death were mourning,
Welcome with thy smiles returning.
     Let thine Alleluia rise !

Raise thy heavy eyelids, Mary,
   See Him living evermore ;
See His countenance how gracious,
   See the wounds for thee He bore.
All the gems on Sion gleaming
Pale before those wounds redeeming.
     Let thine Alleluia rise !

Life is thine for ever, Mary,
   For thy Light is come again ;
And the strength of death is broken,
   Tides of joy fill every vein.

---

[1] Alluding to the belief prevalent in the Middle Ages, that the " woman who was a sinner " (Luke vii.) was the Magdalene.

Far hath fled the night of sorrow,
Love hath brought the blessed morrow.
Let thine Alleluia rise!

SPRING AND THE RESURRECTION.

Trench, p. 153.

ADAM OF ST. VICTOR.

(*Mundi renovatio.*)

The renewal of the world
   Countless new joys bringeth forth;
Christ arising, all things rise,
   Rise with Him from earth.
All the creatures feel their Lord,
Feel His festal light outpour'd.

Fire springs up with motion free,
   Breezes wake up soft and warm;
Water flows abundantly,
   Earth remaineth firm.
All things light now skyward soar,
Solid things are rooted more;
   All things are made new.

Ocean waves, grown tranquil, lie
   Smiling 'neath the heavens serene;
All the air breathes light and fresh,
   Our valley groweth green.
Verdure clothes the arid plain,
Frozen waters gush again,
   At the touch of Spring.

For the frost of death is melted,
   The prince of this world lieth low,
And his empire strong amongst us,
   All is broken now.

Grasping Him in whom alone
He could nothing claim or own,
  His domain he lost.

Paradise is now regain'd,
  Life has vanquish'd death,
And the joys he long had lost
  Man recovereth.
The cherubim, at God's own word,
Turn aside the flaming sword;
The long-lost blessing is restored,
  The closed way open'd free.

SPRING AND EASTER.

Daniel, vol. iii. p. 366.

(*Plaudite cœli.*)

Smile praises, O sky,
  Soft breathe them, O air,
Below and on high,
  And everywhere!
The black troop of storms
  Has yielded to calm;
Tufted blossoms are peeping,
  And early palm.

Arouse thee, O spring;
  Ye flowers, come forth,
With thousand hues tinting
  The soft green earth;
Ye violets tender,
  And sweet roses bright,
Gay Lent-lilies blended
  With pure lilies white.

Sweep, tides of rich music,
    The full veins along;
And pour in full measure,
    Sweet lyres, your song.
Sing, sing, for He liveth,
    He lives, as He said;
The Lord is arisen
    Unharm'd from the dead!

Clap, clap your hands, mountains,
    Ye valleys, resound;
Leap, leap for joy, fountains,
    Ye hills, catch the sound.
All triumph! He liveth,
    He lives, as He said;
The Lord hath arisen
    Unharm'd from the dead!

TO THE HOLY SPIRIT.

Trench, p. 196.

KING ROBERT THE SECOND OF FRANCE—DIED 1031.

(*Veni, Sancte Spiritus.*)

Holy Spirit, come, we pray,
Come from heaven and shed the ray
    Of Thy light divine.

Come, Thou Father of the poor,
Giver from a boundless store,
    Light of hearts, O shine!

Matchless Comforter in woe,
Sweetest Guest the soul can know,
    Living waters blest.

When we weep, our solace sweet,
Coolest shade in summer heat,
    In our labour rest.

Holy and most blessed Light,
Make our inmost spirits bright
    With Thy radiance mild;

For without Thy sacred powers,
Nothing can we own of ours,
    Nothing undefiled.

What is arid, fresh bedew;
What is sordid, cleanse anew;
    Balm on the wounded pour.

What is rigid, gently bend;
On what is cold, Thy fervour send;
    What has stray'd, restore.

To Thine own in every place
Give the sacred sevenfold grace,
    Give Thy faithful this.

Give to virtue its reward,
Safe and peaceful end afford,
    Give eternal bliss.

TO THE HOLY SPIRIT.

Trench, p. 175.

ADAM OF ST. VICTOR.

Veni, Creator Spiritus, Spiritus Recreator.)

Come, Creator-Spirit high,
    Re-creating ever;
Given and giving from the sky,
    Thou the Gift and Giver.

Thou the Law within us writ,
Finger Thou that writeth it,
  Inspired and Inspirer!

With Thy sevenfold graces good
  Sevenfold gifts be given.
For sevenfold beatitude,
  And petitions seven.[1]
Thou the pure, unstained snow,
That shall never sullied flow;
Fire that burns not though it glow;
Wrestler who no fear canst know,
  Giving words of wisdom.

Kindle Thou Thyself in us,
  Thou both Light and Fire;
Thou Thyself still into us,
  Breath of Life, inspire!
Thou the Ray and Thou the Sun,
Sent and Sender, Thee we own;
Of the Blessed Three in One,
Thee we, suppliant, call upon.
  Save us now and ever.

ON THE DAY OF JUDGMENT.

Trench, p. 296.

THOMAS OF CELANO—THIRTEENTH CENTURY.

(*Dies iræ, Dies illa.*)

Lo, the Day of wrath, the Day!
Earth and heaven melt away,
David and the Sibyl say.

---

[1] The seven petitions in the Lord's Prayer.

Stoutest hearts with fear shall quiver,
When to Him who erreth never
All must strict account deliver.

Lo, the trumpet's wondrous pealing,
Flung through each sepulchral dwelling,
All before the throne compelling!

Nature shrinks appall'd, and Death
When the dead regain their breath:
To the Judge each answereth.

Then the Written Book is set,
All things are contain'd in it,
Thence each learns his sentence meet.

When the Judge appears again,
Hidden things shall be made plain,
Nothing unavenged remain.

What shall I, unworthy plead?
Who for me will intercede,
When the just will mercy need?

King of dreadful majesty,
Who sav'st the saved, of mercy free,
Fount of pity, save Thou me!

Think of me, good Lord, I pray,
Who trodd'st for me the bitter way,
Nor forsake me in that Day.

Weary sat'st Thou seeking me,
Diedst redeeming on the Tree;
Not in vain such toil can be!

Judge avenging, let me win
Free remission of my sin,
Ere that dreadful Day begin.

Sinful, o'er my sins I groan,
Guilt my crimson'd face must own;
Spare, O God, Thy suppliant one!

Mary was by Thee forgiven,
To the thief Thou open'dst heaven;
Hope to me, too, Thou hast given.

All unworthy is my prayer;
Gracious One, be gracious there;
From that quenchless fire, oh spare!

Place Thou me at Thy right hand,
'Mongst Thy sheep, oh make me stand,
Far from the convicted band.

When the accursed condemn'd shall be,
Doom'd to keenest flames by Thee,
'Midst the blessed call Thou me.

Contrite suppliant, I pray,
Ashes on my heart I lay,
Care Thou for me in that Day.

THE RESURRECTION DAY.

Trench, p. 288.

FROM A POEM OF THE TWELFTH CENTURY, BY AN UNKNOWN AUTHOR, BEGINNING "CUM REVOLVO TOTO CORDE."

(*Dies illa, Dies vitæ.*)

Lo, the Day, the Day of Life!
Day of unimagined light,
Day when Death itself shall die,
And there shall be no more night.

Steadily that Day approacheth,
    When the just shall find their rest,
When the wicked cease from troubling,
    And the patient reign most blest.

See the King desired for ages,
    By the just expected long;
Long implored, at length he hasteth,
    Cometh with salvation strong.

Oh, how past all utterance happy,
    Sweet and joyful it will be
When they who, unseen, have loved Him,
    Jesus face to face shall see!

In that Day, how good and pleasant,
    This poor world to have despised!
And how mournful, and how bitter,
    Dear that lost world to have prized!

Blessed, then, earth's patient mourners,
    Who for Christ have toil'd and died,
Driven by the world's rough pressure
    In those mansions to abide!

There shall be no sighs or weeping,
    Not a shade of doubt or fear;
No old age, no want or sorrow,
    Nothing sick or lacking there.

There the peace will be unbroken,
    Deep and solemn joy be shed;
Youth in fadeless flower and freshness,
    And salvation perfected.

What will be the bliss and rapture
    None can dream and none can tell,
There to reign among the angels,
    In that heavenly home to dwell.

To those realms, just Judge, oh call me;
    Deign to open that blest gate,
Thou whom, seeking, looking, longing,
    I, with eager hope, await!

THE JOYS OF HEAVEN.

Trench, p. 315.

CARDINAL PETER DAMIANI—1003-1072.

(*Ad perennis vitæ fontem mens sitivit arida.*)

In the Fount of life perennial parch'd hearts fain their thirst would slake,
And the soul, in flesh imprison'd, longs her prison walls to break;
Exile, seeking, sighing, yearning, in her fatherland to wake.

When with cares oppress'd and sorrows, only groans her grief can tell,
Then she contemplates the glory which she lost when first she fell;
Present evil but the memory of the vanish'd good can swell.

Who can utter what the pleasures and the peace unbroken are,
Where arise the pearly mansions, shedding silvery light afar,
Festive seats and golden roofs, which glitter like the evening star!

Wholly of fair stones most precious are those radiant structures made;
With pure gold, like glass transparent, are those shining streets inlaid;
Nothing that defiles can enter, nothing that can soil or fade.

Stormy winter, burning summer, rage within those regions never,
But perpetual bloom of roses and unfading spring for ever;
Lilies gleam, the crocus glows, and dropping balms their scents deliver.

Honey pure, and greenest pastures, this the land of promise is;
Liquid odours soft distilling, perfumes breathing on the breeze;
Fruits immortal cluster always on the leafy fadeless trees.

There no moon shines chill and changing, there no stars with twinkling ray,
For the Lamb of that blest city is at once the Sun and Day;
Night and time are known no longer, day shall never fade away.

There the saints like suns are radiant, like the sun at dawn they glow;
Crownèd victors after conflict, all their joys together flow,
And secure they count the battles where they fought the prostrate foe.

Every stain of flesh is cleansèd, every strife is left behind,
Spiritual are their bodies, perfect unity of mind;
Dwelling in deep peace for ever, no offence or grief they find.

Putting off their mortal vesture, in their Source their souls they steep;
Truth by actual vision learning, on its form their gaze they keep,
Drinking from the living Fountain draughts of living waters deep.

Time, with all its alternations, enters not those hosts among;
Glorious, wakeful, blest, no shade of chance or change o'er them is flung;
Sickness cannot touch the deathless, nor old age the ever young.

There their being is eternal, things that cease have ceased to be;
All corruption there has perish'd, there they flourish strong and free;
Thus mortality is swallow'd up of life eternally.

Nought from them is hidden, knowing Him to whom all things are known;
All the spirit's deep recesses, sinless, to each other shown,—
Unity of will and purpose, heart and mind for ever one.

Diverse as their varied labours the rewards to each that fall,
But Love what she loves in others, evermore her own doth call;
Thus the several joy of each becomes the common joy of all.

Where the body is, there ever are the eagles gather'd,
For the saints and for the angels one most blessed feast is spread,—
Citizens of either country living on the self-same bread.

Ever fill'd, and ever seeking, what they have they still desire;
Hunger there shall fret them never, nor satiety shall tire,—
Still enjoying whilst aspiring, in their joy they still aspire.

There the new song, new for ever, those melodious voices
    sing ;
Ceaseless streams of fullest music through those blessed
    regions ring ;
Crownèd victors ever bringing praises worthy of the
    King !

Blessed who the King of heaven in His beauty thus
    behold,
And beneath His throne rejoicing see the universe
    unfold,—
Sun and moon, and stars and planets, radiant in His
    light unroll'd !

Christ, the Palm of faithful victors ! of that city make
    me free ;
When my warfare shall be ended, to its mansions lead
    Thou me,—
Grant me, with its happy inmates, sharer of Thy gifts to
    be !

Let Thy soldier, still contending, still be with Thy
    strength supplied ;
Thou wilt not deny the quiet when the arms are laid
    aside ;
Make me meet with Thee for ever in that country to
    abide !

ON THE JOYS OF HEAVEN.

Trench, p. 321.

THOMAS À KEMPIS—1380–1471.

High the angel choirs are raising
    Heart and voice in harmony ;
The Creator King still praising,
    Whom in beauty there they see.

Sweetest strains, from soft harps stealing;
Trumpets, notes of triumph pealing:
Radiant wings and white stoles gleaming,
Up the steps of glory streaming;
Where the heavenly bells are ringing,
Holy, holy, holy! singing
   To the mighty Trinity!
Holy, holy, holy! crying;
For all earthly care and sighing
   In that city cease to be!

Every voice is there harmonious,
Praising God in hymns symphonious;
Love each heart with light infolding,
As they stand in peace beholding
   There the Triune Deity!
Whom adore the seraphim,
   Aye with love eternal burning;
Venerate the cherubim,
   To their Fount of honour turning;
   Whilst angelic thrones adoring
     Gaze upon His majesty.

Oh how beautiful that region,
And how fair that heavenly legion,
   Where thus men and angels blend!
Glorious will that city be,
Full of deep tranquillity,
   Light and peace from end to end!
All the happy dwellers there
   Shine in robes of purity,
   Keep the law of charity,
   Bound in firmest unity;
Labour finds them not, nor care.

Ignorance can ne'er perplex,
Nothing tempt them, nothing vex;
Joy and health their fadeless blessing,
Always all things good possessing.

THE BETTER COUNTRY—THAT IS, THE HEAVENLY.

FROM THE RHYTHM OF BERNARD.

Trench, p. 304.

BERNARD OF CLUGNY—TWELFTH CENTURY.[1]

(*Hic breve vivitur, hic breve plangitur, hic breve fletur.*)

Here brief is the sighing,
And brief is the crying,
  For brief is the life!
The life there is endless,
The joy there is endless,
  And ended the strife.

What joys are in heaven?
To whom are they given?
  Ah! what? and to whom
The stars to the earth-born,
"Best robes" to the sin-worn,
  The crown for the doom!

O country the fairest!
Our country, the dearest!
  We press towards thee!
O Sion the golden!
Our eyes now are holden,
  Thy light till we see:

Thy crystalline ocean,
Unvexed by commotion,
  Thy fountain of life;

---

[1] Born at Morlaix, in Brittany, but of English parents.

Thy deep peace unspoken,
Pure, sinless, unbroken,—
　Thy peace beyond strife :

Thy meek saints all glorious,
Thy martyrs victorious,
　Who suffer no more ;
Thy halls full of singing,
Thy hymns ever ringing
　Along thy safe shore.

Like the lily for whiteness,
Like the jewel for brightness,
　Thy vestments, O Bride !
The Lamb ever with thee,
The Bridegroom is with thee,—
　With thee to abide !

We know not, we know not,
All human words show not,
　The joys we may reach ;
The mansions preparing,
The joys for our sharing,
　The welcome for each.

O Sion the golden !
My eyes still are holden
　Thy light till I see ;
And deep in thy glory,
Unveiled then before me,
　My King, look on Thee

ST. STEPHEN'S DAY.

Trench, p. 212.

ADAM OF ST. VICTOR.

(*Heri mundus exultavit.*)

Yesterday the happy earth
Peal'd her grateful praises forth,
   Keeping Christ's nativity;
Yesterday the angel throng
Met the King of heaven with song,
   And with high festivity.

Protomartyr in the strife,
Noble both in faith and life,
   Wonder-working gifts receiving,
Thou, O Stephen, 'neath that Light,
Triumphedst with heavenly might,
   Braving all the unbelieving!

Light's foes, like wild beasts at bay,
Quivering crouch to seize their prey,
   By Thy words of truth heart-stung:
Lying witnesses they bring,
Viper's brood with viper's sting,
   Poisonous and lying tongue.

Noble wrestler, yield to none,
For thy victory must be won;
   Stephen, struggle bravely through!
Those false witnesses refute,
Satan's synagogue confute,
   With thy holy speech and true.

From heaven thy Witness watcheth thee,
True and faithful Witness He,
   Witness of thine innocence;

Stephen, Crown'd One, is thy name!
Light the torture and the shame
   For that crown of light intense.

For that crown that cannot wither,
Press through these brief torments thither!
   Triumph shall reward thy strife:
Death is thy nativity,
And thy sufferings' close shall be
   The beginning of thy life!

The Holy Spirit filleth him!
And his sight no more is dim,
   Piercing heaven with dying eyes;
He sees the glory of his God,
Sigheth for that blest abode,
   Pressing forward to the prize.

Jesus on God's right hand standing,
Standing and for thee contending,
   Stephen, lift thine eyes and see!
Jesus to thy vision given,
Christ for thee unclosing heaven;
   Call on Him, He watcheth thee!

Then his spirit he commends
To that Saviour, Friend of friends,
For whose sake he deems it sweet
All that rage and pain to meet,
   Sweet to die beneath those stones!
Saul the murderers' raiment keepeth,
In that crime his heart he steepeth,
   As his own each blow he owns.

Lest the sin to them be laid
By whose hands his blood was shed,
Kneeling down, for them he pray'd,
   Rendering pity for the wrong.

Thus in Christ he calmly slept
Who so true to Christ had kept,
And with Christ he reigneth ever,
Ever since, and still for ever,
   First-fruits of the martyr throng!

ON AFFLICTION.

Trench, p. 219.

FROM A HYMN ON THE MARTYRDOM OF ST. LAWRENCE, BY ADAM OF ST. VICTOR.

(*Sicut chorda musicorum.*)

As the harp-strings only render
   All their treasures of sweet sound,
All their music, glad or tender,
   Firmly struck and tightly bound:

So the hearts of Christians owe
   Each its deepest, sweetest strain,
To the pressure firm of woe,
   And the tension tight of pain.

Spices crush'd their pungence yield,
   Trodden scents their sweets respire;
Would you have its strength reveal'd,
   Cast the incense in the fire:

Thus the crush'd and broken frame
   Oft doth sweetest graces yield,
And through suffering, toil, and shame,
From the martyr's keenest flame
   Heavenly incense is distill'd!

ALLELUIA DULCE CARMEN.

Daniel, vol. i. p. 261. CCLXXIII.

Alleluia! sweetest music, voice of everlasting joy!
Alleluia is the language which the heavenly choirs employ,
As they ever sing to God, in that pure and blest abode.

Alleluia! joyful mother, true Jerusalem above!
Alleluia is the music which the happy children love:
Exiles, tears our songs must steep; oft by Babel's streams we weep.

Alleluia cannot ever be our joyous psalm below;
Alleluia!—sin will cross it often here with tones of woe;
Many a mournful hour we know, when our tears for sin must flow.

Therefore, 'mid our fears still praising, grant us, Blessed Trinity,
Thy true Paschal Feast hereafter in the heavenly home to see,
Where our song shall ever be, Alleluia unto Thee!

FROM A SEQUENCE IN COMMEMORATION OF ST. MARY MAGDALENE.

The sinner condemns his fellow-sinner. Thou who knowest no sin receivest the penitent, purifiest the impure, lovest that Thou mayest make beautiful.

At the close of this chapter may be placed, though passing the limits of the Middle Ages, a hymn attributed to St. Francis Xavier, and two sonnets by Michael Angelo:

BY MICHAEL ANGELO BUONAROTTI.

SONETTO XLIX.

Scarco d'una importuna e grave salma,
Signore eterno, e dal monda disciolto
Qual fragil legno a te stanco mi volto
Dall' orribil procella in dolce calma.

Le spine i chiodi e l'una e l'altra palma
Col tuo benigno umíl lacero volto
Prometton grazia di pentirsi molto,
E speme di salute alla trist' alma.

Non miri con giustizia il divin lume
Moi fallo, o l'oda il tuo sacrato orecchio
Nè in quel si volge il braccio tuo severo.

Tuo sangue lavi l'empio mio costume,
E più m'abbondi, quanto io son più vecchio,
Di pronta aita e di perdono intero.

A M. GIORGIO VASARI.

Giunto è già 'l corso della vita mia
Con tempestosa mar per fragil barca
Al comun porto, ov'a render si varca
Giusta ragion d'ogni opra trista e pia;

Onde l'affettuosa fantasia
Che l'arte si fece idolo e monarca,
Conosco ben quant'era d'error carca;
L'errore è ciò che l'uom quaggiù desia.

I pensier miei già de' mie' danni lieti,
Che fian or s'a due morti m'avoicino?
L'uno m'è certa e l'altra mi minaccia.

Nè pinger nè scolpir fia più che queti
L'anima volta a quell' amor divino,
Ch'aperse a prender noi 'n croce le braccia.

Translations by John S. Harford.

SONNET XLIX.

From a vexatious heavy load set free,
Eternal Lord! and from the world unloosed,
Wearied to Thee I turn, like a frail bark,
'Scaped from fierce storms, into a placid sea.
The thorns, the nails, the one and the other hand,
Together with Thine aspect, meek, benign,
And mangled, pledge the grace to mourning souls
Of deep repentance and salvation's hope.
View not my sins in the condemning light
Of justice strict; avert Thine awful ear,
Nor stretch forth on me Thine avenging arm.
May Thy blood wash my guilt and sins away;
As age creeps on, may it abound the more
With timely aid, and full forgiveness!

And in his eighty-third year—

TO VASARI.

Time my frail bark o'er a rough ocean guides
Swift to that port where all must touch that live,
And of their actions, good or evil, give
A strict account, where Truth supreme presides.
As to gay Fancy, in which Art confides,
And even her idol and her monarch makes,
Full well I know how largely it partakes
Of error; but frail man in error prides.
Thy thoughts, once prompt round hurtful things to twine,
What are they now when two dread deaths are near?
The one impends, the other shakes his spear.
Painting and Sculpture's aid in vain I crave;
My one sole refuge is that Love Divine
Which from the Cross stretch'd forth its arms to save.

ORATIO AD DEUM.

FRANCIS XAVIER.

O Deus, ego amo te ;
   Nec amo te ut salves me,
Aut quia non amantes te
   Æterno punis igne.

Tu, Tu, mi Jesu, totum me
   Amplexus es in cruce ;
Tulisti clavos, lanceam,
   Multamque ignominiam,

Innumeros dolores,
   Sudores et angores,
Ac mortem, et hæc propter me,
   Ac pro me peccatore.

Cur igitur non amem te,
   O Jesu amantissime !
Non, ut in cœlo salves me,
   Aut ne æternum damnes me,

Nec proemii ullius spe ;
   Sed sicut tu amasti me.
Sic amo et amabo te,
   Solum quia Rex meus es,
   Et solum quia Deus es.

O God ! my heart is fixed on Thee,
Not that Thou may'st deliver me,
Nor because those who love not Thee
   In quenchless fire must languish ;
But Thou, my Saviour, on the tree,
Embracedst me with mercy free,
For me didst bitter mockings bear,
For me the torturing nails and spear,

Much shame and speechless anguish,
And death itself; and all for me,
　　And in my stead, a sinner.
How therefore can I not love Thee,
O worthy best beloved to be!
Not for the hope of joy in heaven,
Nor fear lest I to hell be driven,
Nor, O my freely loving Lord!
For any promise of reward,
But all because Thou lovedst me!
Thus love I Thee with steadfast heart
Only because my King Thou art,
　　And because Thou art God.

CHAPTER IX

THE HYMNS OF GERMANY

O mere improvement in correctness of doctrine could have stirred the heart of Europe as the Reformation did. The assertion of the " right of private judgment" might have shattered Christendom with a war of independence, but could not have brought peace to one heart. Had not the Serpent asserted it long ago in Eden ? The clearest statements of the doctrine of justification by faith could not in themselves have swept away all the barriers superstition had been building up for centuries between man and God. Many of the theologians of the Middle Ages doubtless understood that doctrine. The Reformation was not the mere statement of a positive dogma, still less was it the mere assertion of a negative right ; it was the revealing of a Person; it was the unveiling of a heart. It was the fresh revelation through the Bible to the heart of one man, and through him to the hearts of thousands, that "God is love," and "hath so loved the world;" that a heart of infinite love embraces

us on every side, and rules in heaven. It was at once the result of the reaction against abuses acknowledged by all good men on all sides, and the fruit of "those countless kindred minds" which had "thronged the cloister for a thousand years" and were to "issue at length in German mysticism and Luther."[1]

"The French mystics of the twelfth century and their followers, in reaction from the somewhat thin rationalism of their day, developed an emotional rather than an intellectual type of mysticism—which with all its fervour and beauty was not widely influential on the progress of thought. But with the German mystics, Eckhart, Tauler, Suso, the case was different. To begin with, the time was more fully ripe for their effective appearance. And further, they sprang from the great preaching order, and laboured, under the exigencies of the pulpit, to bring their meaning home to the mass of men; while the fact, that both preachers and hearers were of the subjective Teutonic race, gave that intellectual cast to their teaching which enabled it to influence all subsequent thought. We are only concerned here with their contribution to the development of personality; which consisted in emphasizing the intimacy and immediacy of the union between the soul and God. This was no more than had been taught in the earlier ages of Christianity, or than was justified in the philosophy of Albert the Great and St. Thomas Aquinas.

"But practically the tendency of the mediæval

[1] Illingworth, "Bampton Lectures," p. 16, Personality Human and Divine.

church, with its over-use of sacerdotal and saintly mediation, had been to exaggerate the distance between God and man. Hence the significance of the mystical movement. But mysticism has always had its attendant danger—the danger of seeking union with God by obliteration of human limitations and human attributes on the one hand, and on the other of under-estimating the human sense of guilt, that awful guardian of our personal identity. Hence, though it begins by deepening our sense of individuality, it often ends by drifting, both morally and intellectually, towards Pantheism in which all individuality is lost. From this danger with all their merits, the German mystics were not wholly free. And consequently Luther, who was profoundly influenced by them, without falling into their error, became the most effectual exponent of their central thought.

"In saying this we are not concerned with his theology in general, but with the central thought which lay at the root of it all; a thought which he expressed in a more intelligible and perhaps, on the whole, a more guarded way than Eckhart, and for which he consequently secured a popularity such as Eckhart could never have attained. That thought was the natural affinity of the human soul, through all its sin, for God; and of God for the human soul; and the consequent possibility of an immediate relation between the two. He turned, as Dormer puts it, from the metaphysical to the moral attributes of God and man, culminating as they do in love; and proclaimed that here was the only ground for an intimate and in a measure intelligible union of the two. For it is the nature of a God whose essence is love to communicate Himself, and the nature of a man whose essence is the desire for love to be receptive of that communication (capax deitatis). The famous phrase 'justification by faith' is an attempt to express this thought. 'Faith,' he says in one place, 'is, if I may use the expression, creative of divinity; not, of course, in the substance of God, but in ourselves!'[1]

"Faith has, strictly speaking, no object but Christ . . . and it is this faith which lays hold of Christ and is clothed with Him (ornatur) which justifies."[2] This intimacy and immediacy of possible union between the soul and God was, of course, no theological novelty; but it had long vanished from the popular religion.

"Luther re-emphasized it with a vehemence to which the circumstances of the age contributed yet further emphasis; and above all, he proclaimed it the basis of spiritual independence; the soul, which is the slave of God, being thereby free from all other slavery, to religious or philosophic authority and external means of grace. The freedom of the human spirit through union with God became thus a familiar thought, a recognized principle, a controversial commonplace, in the mouths of many who had no inner experience of its truth. But however paradoxically stated, abused, exaggerated, misapplied, its publication made an epoch in the world. It had previously been an esoteric doctrine. Luther proclaimed it from the housetop; and in so doing dignified and deepened the whole sense of per-

[1] Luther, in Gal. ii. 16.   [2] *Ibid.* ii. 20.

sonality in man." "Christ's victory," Luther writes, "is the overcoming of the law, of sin, our flesh, the world, the devil, death, hell, and all evils; and this victory He hath given unto us." "Although, then, these tyrants and these enemies of ours do accuse us and make us afraid, yet can they not drive us to despair, nor condemn us; for Christ, whom God the Father hath raised from the dead, is our righteousness and victory."

Again, on the words, "Who hath given Himself for our sins," he writes (referring to the efforts of Satan to drive us to despair on account of our sins): "Against this temptation we urge these words of the Apostle, in the which he gives a very good and true definition of Christ in this manner, 'Christ is the Son of God and of the Virgin, delivered and put to death for our sins.' Here, if the devil urge any other definition of Christ, say thou, The definition and the thing defined are false. I speak not this without cause, for I know what urgeth me to be so earnest, that we should learn to define Christ out of the words of Paul. For, indeed, Christ is no cruel Exactor, but a Forgiver of the sins of the whole world. Wherefore, if thou be a sinner, as indeed we all are, set not Christ down upon the rainbow as a Judge, lest thou shouldst be terrified and despair of His mercy, but take hold of this true definition, namely, that Christ, the Son of God and of the Virgin, is a Person, not that terrifieth, not that afflicteth, not that condemneth us of sin, not that demandeth of us an account for our life evil passed, but hath given Himself for our sins, and with one oblation hath put away the sins of the whole world, hath fastened them upon the Cross, and put them clean out by Himself." "Hold this fast, and suffer not thyself by any means to be drawn away from this most sweet definition of Christ, which rejoiceth even the very angels in heaven; that is to say, that Christ, according to the true definition, is no Moses, no lawgiver, no tyrant, but a Mediator for sins, a free giver of grace, righteousness, and life."

Again: "Christ, then, is no Moses, no exactor, no giver of laws, but a giver of grace, a Saviour, and one that is full of mercy; briefly, He is nothing else but infinite mercy and goodness, freely given, and bountifully giving unto us. And thus shall you paint out Christ in His right colours. If you suffer Him any otherwise to be painted out unto you, when temptation and trouble cometh you shall soon be overthrown. Now, as it is the greatest knowledge and cunning that Christians can have thus to define Christ, so of all things it is the hardest. Christ, therefore, in very deed is a lover of those which are in trouble and anguish, in sin and death; such a lover as gave Himself for us, who is also our High Priest, that is to say, a Mediator between God and us miserable and wretched sinners." Again: "I am covered under the shadow of Christ's wings, as is the chicken under the wing of the hen, and dwell, without all fear, under that most ample heaven of the forgiveness of sins." Again: "Feeling Thy terrors, O Lord, I plunge my conscience in the wounds, blood, death, resurrection, and victory of my Saviour, Christ. Beside Him I will see nothing, I will hear nothing."

These extracts are given thus at length as enfolding the Reformation. It was morning again in Germany, and, to welcome such a morning, it was no wonder that there poured forth such a chorus of song.

The hymn-literature of Germany is too rich to be given an idea of in a portion of a book; and many admirable translations have already appeared, to which the reader may easily refer. There is, besides, a peculiar freshness and purity, an unconscious power and sublimity in these hymns, which make their translation peculiarly difficult. Simplicity, in a translation, is apt to look self-conscious, and so to become that worst of affectations, the affectation of simplicity. A very few illustrations, therefore, must suffice for this volume, with a brief sketch of the general character of the hymns and of their writers.

In comparing these with those of the Middle Ages, the first thing that strikes us is the far greater variety in the subjects of the hymns and in the position of the writers. Sacred song has issued again from the narrow walls of the cloister to the workshop, the harvest-field, and the home. There are hymns for various family joys and family sorrows, hymns for toil and for battle, for the sick-bed and the way-side.

Especially numerous are those which express trust in God in trial or conflict, which speak of Him, like the old Hebrew psalms, as a Rock, a Fortress, and a Deliverer. Spiritual songs have once more become battle-songs. The intricate intertwinings of rhyme and the lingering cadences of the later mediæval hymns vanish, and the inspiring decision of martial music rings through them once more. They are songs to march to, reviving the fainting strength after many an hour of weary journeying; blasts of the priests' trumpets, before which many a stronghold has fallen; chants of trust and of triumph, which must often have reverberated from the very gates of heaven as they accompanied the departing spirit thither, and mingled with the new song of the great multitude inside.

The hymns of Germany have been her true national Liturgy. In England the worship of the Reformed Church was linked to that of past ages by the prayer-book; in Germany by the hymn-book. The music and the hymns of the mediæval Church were not separated by so definite a barrier from the psalmody of the German Evangelical Churches as from ours, but floated on into it, the old blending with the new. The miner's son, who in his school days had carolled for bread before the doors of the burghers of Eisenach, remembered the old melodies, when the hearts of his people were looking to him for the "bread which satisfieth," and gave forth out of his treasure-house things new and old. The great Reformer of the German Church was also her first great singer. Luther gave the German people their hymn-book as well as their Bible. He brought over some of the best old hymns into the new worship, not word by word in the ferry-boat of a literal translation, but entire and living, like Israel through the Jordan, when the priests' feet, bearing the ark, swept back the waters.

Yet, as in his theses affixed to the church door at Wittenberg, so in his hymns, Luther seems to have had no plan of writing for a nation, but simply to have spoken out the irrepressible emotions and overpowering convictions of his own heart, come of it what might. "Here stand I, I can no other; God help me, Amen," breathes through his hymns as well as his confession. The great battle-song of the German Church—his "Eine feste Burg ist unser Gott"—was said to have come into his heart on his way to the Diet at Worms. Its truths were certainly there then, whatever antiquarian research may prove about the date when they were written down. "Out of the depths I cry to Thee," he sang when recovering from a fainting-fit, brought on by the intensity of spiritual conflict; and when at last his dead body was borne through Halle, on its way to its last resting-place at Wittenberg, his countrymen thronged into the church where it was laid, and amidst their tears and sobs, sang that hymn beside it. His sweet Christmas hymn, "Vom Himmel hoch da komm ich her," was written for his little son Hans. "The poet had the child's heart in his breast." From the old Latin psalmody he gave a free rhymed translation of the "Te Deum" and several of the Ambrosian hymns. The funeral hymn, "Media in vita in morte sumus,"[1] composed by Notker, a monk of St. Gall, A.D. 900 (the first line of which appears in our burial-service), he poured forth anew in three verses,

---

[1] This hymn may be thus translated:—

"In the midst of life we are in death;
What helper shall we seek but thee, O Lord,
Who art justly incensed against our sins!
Holy God, Holy Mighty One, Holy and Merciful Saviour,
Deliver us not to bitter death!"

and infused into it a tone of confidence and hope very faintly audible in the original.

Just as the first recorded hymn of the Church was called forth by the first persecution, when the place was shaken where the disciples were met, and they were all "filled with the Holy Ghost," it is interesting to find that Luther's first hymn was called forth by the death of "two martyrs of Christ, burned at Brussels by the Sophists."

The hymn of his, of which a translation is given at the close of this chapter, is in the early hymn-books called "An Evangelical Hymn, to be sung before or after the sermon;" and in one of those books, "An Evangelical Song, very comforting to the sinner." In the original, every verse of it seems at once to tremble with tears of joy, and to ring with the peal of victory.

To give a series of biographies of German hymn-writers would be to write the Church history of Germany. To the three thousand and sixty-six hymns selected in the "Liederschatz" of Albrecht Knapp is appended a list of four hundred writers, with brief biographical notices of each. It is this multiplicity of hymn-writers which, in regarding hymns as the voice of Christian life, gives its great interest to German hymnology. The German hymn-book is no mere series of metrical compositions compiled by a few orthodox divines; nor is it a collection of the religious poems of a few poets. It is the utterance of the heart of the German people, of those whom faith in Him who is invisible has made singers. It is emphatically a fragment of the great song of the Church universal. For the first time in the history of hymns, since Mary the mother of Jesus sang her song of joy, the names of women appear among the singers. Louisa Henrietta, born Princess of Orange, wife of the Great Elector, Frederick William of Brandenburg, poured out her hope and trust in a Resurrection Hymn, which, as a rock of faith, stands beside the hymns of Luther himself, or Paul Gerhard. During the two hundred years which have elapsed since the Christian princess breathed her heart into those verses, how many souls have been breathed out to God with its words falling from the dying lips! A translation is attempted in this volume.

In the biographical list of writers given by Albrecht Knapp, many names occur in strange juxtaposition. Reformed and Lutheran are there, side by side, singing parts of the same song; those who suffered for Lutheranism, and those who suffered for Calvinism, and also those who contended for both; though, probably, more of the sufferers than the combatants. Too often the choir of the Church on earth is built like the chapels of prisons, on the separate system; each worshipper is walled out from his neighbour. In these hymn-books (as we believe it will be in heaven) the barriers are broken down, and we see Luther's hymns used with those of a Zwinglian, and the hymns of a Roman Catholic mystic, such as Angelus, with those of a Reformed divine.

In the list referred to, (at the end of Albrecht Knapp's "Liederschatz"), between the names of the Electress Louisa Henrietta and the Countess Ludæmilia Elizabeth of Schwarzburg-Rudolstadt, occurs that of Löwenstern, "a saddler's son;" then

Dr. Martin Luther; a little below, Maria, Queen of Hungary, Melanchthon, and Joachim Neander, Calvinistic preacher at Bremen.

Among the names otherwise distinguished are those of Franke, founder of the Orphan House at Halle, Arndt, Claudius, the Moravian missionary Leonhard Dober, who offered to be sold as a slave in order to preach to the slaves in the West Indies, Klopstock, the Krummachers, Lavater, the Margrave Albert of Brandenburg, Spener, Novalis, De la Motte Fouqué, many carpenters, shoemakers, Princes and Princesses, and the great king Gustavus.

Among the most distinguished names of those known chiefly through their hymns are Paul Gerhard, Gerhard Tersteegen, Angelus, Schmolke, and Hiller. Of these Paul Gerhard is held to be the greatest. He lived in the seventeenth century, in Saxony and in Prussia, and died A.D. 1676, at the age of seventy, after a life of many outward trials and intense inward conflicts, of which (Albrecht Knapp writes) one of his contemporaries said, " they would naturally have caused him rather to cry with pain than to sing." No doubt it is the suppressed cry of pain which gives the peculiar depth to his song of victory. One of his most beautiful hymns—" Wake up, my heart, and sing "—was composed on the steps of the altar at Lübben, after a night of anguish. Every line of it breathes the deepest trust and peace. Like St. Paul, he comforted others with the comfort wherewith he himself had been comforted of God! Like so many who have borne the most cheering messages to the Church, the consoler had first been the sufferer. This kind of song is only learned on the battle-field. You feel in every verse of Gerhard's that his is proved armour.

The hymns of Tersteegen, one of which is the well-known "Thou hidden love of God," are more quiet and meditative. He lived in the beginning of the eighteenth century, a life of deep, still communion with God, choosing the occupation of a ribbon-maker on account of its tranquillity, and, from his humble home, shed a blessed influence over great numbers who sought his counsel. His light seems to have shone and been diffused, not by express effort, but simply because he dwelt himself so much in the light. His piety was the fountain of his poetry, and the deep beauty of his heavenly thoughts glows through the rudeness of the earthen vessel which holds them. He died at Mühlheim on the Rühr, A.D. 1769, at the age of seventy-six.

The German hymns range through three centuries, but may be divided into three principal groups, linked together by many scattered compositions which intervene, and seem to carry on the one unbroken song. These groups would naturally concentrate round the periods of the Reformation, the great religious struggle of the Thirty Years' War, and the revival of religion in the days of Franke and Zinzendorf through the earlier half of the eighteenth century.

To the first period belong about twenty hymn-writers, gathering round Luther as the leader of the choir. In our English hymn-books we have not one composition corresponding with this earliest burst of German song. This primary formation, with its massive strength and its mountain ranges, upheaved by the great inward fire of the Reformation, is with us altogether wanting. And the deficiency is significant. The Reformation reached our country at first only in vibrations from the great central movement in Saxony. Before the evangelical faith had struck root in the heart of the nation, Mary ascended the throne. Then, from one country town to another, the gospel was spread from the stakes of the few who were ready to die for it. During Elizabeth's reign the newly-retranslated English Bible, with its inspired psalms and hymns, and the old Prayer-book, in which Collect and Te Deum now shone forth again, disencumbered of the errors which had hidden them, and unveiled from their foreign disguise, seemed enough for the wants of the people. And thus our hymn literature is at least a century less ancient than that of Germany.

The next great group of German hymns may be gathered around Paul Gerhard, and includes the period of the Thirty Years' War, when Germany was torn asunder, not only by the great religious war between Gustavus Adolphus and the Emperor, but by bitter internal dissensions between Lutheran and Calvinist,—devastated by the fierce and lawless soldiery of Tilly and Wallenstein, and by the famine and pestilence which followed, like vultures, in their train. It was a time of almost unparalleled misery for Germany, and was also her richest harvest-time for sacred song. In number, the known hymn-writers of the seventeenth century were more than a hundred; a list which, allowing for the perspective of time, may be considerably larger than the hundred and sixty of the succeeding century. The distance of two centuries gradually drops below the horizon all but the higher summits of the range, so that the hundred may probably represent twice the number.

Amidst wasted lands and bloody battle-fields, and from homes smitten by worse desolations, the song of faith and hope rose steadily up to God, in tones which only grew deeper as everything on earth grew darker. To this century belong the name of Angelus, and that of Paul Gerhard, the David of the German psalter.

Corresponding to this group, we have in England the names of George Herbert, Richard Baxter, and Bishop Ken.

Through the latter half of the seventeenth and the commencement of the eighteenth century, Spener began, amidst much opposition, his *collegia pietatis*, or meetings of Christians for reading the Scriptures and prayer. He wrote many hymns; and after him followed Jacob Franke, that man of faith who, without pecuniary resources of his own, built the Orphan House of Halle, and was the source of spiritual blessings to so many. Then came Count Zinzendorf, his young heart glowing with love to Christ, setting apart in his estate, near Dresden, a house of refuge (Herrnhut) for the exiled Protestants of Bohemia and Moravia; with all the wide-spread harvest of good which sprang from that offering, missions in the West Indies and Greenland, and the revival of the missionary spirit everywhere.

The deep love to his Master which was Count

Zinzendorf's one characteristic [1] glows in his hymns, some of which were improvised by him during the public services of the Church, like the spiritual songs of earlier days. The Moravian Brethren lived in an atmosphere of music and song more than any other branch of the Church, and no doubt some of their hymns cannot be acquitted from the charge of childishness and sentimental exaggeration; but the emotions which were tempered by practical activity such as theirs must continually have been brought back to a healthy tone. The hearts which poured forth their love on earth in such missions as the Moravians began and still patiently carry on, could not but have poured forth their devotions to heaven in deep and genuine praises. When the work was so real, the song which cheered it must, in the main, have been genuine and healthy; and although there is in these hymns of the eighteenth century more of a subjective character than in the two earlier groups (especially than in that of the Reformation), more dwelling on the feelings of the worshipper, yet these feelings seem to have been true in nature and object.

During this period Tersteegen continued to sing his tranquil, contemplative songs, dwelling apart and bathing his spirit in the depths of the "hidden love of God." His hymns, however, can scarcely be said to belong characteristically to any period.

Contemporary, in England, with his band of singers, were the Wesleys, Toplady, Cowper, Newton, and many others connected with the evangelical revival of the eighteenth century.

[1] "Ich habe eine Passion," he said, "und das ist Er; nur Er."

The six hymns selected for translation at the close of this chapter are taken from these three periods. One is by Luther, one by the Electress Louisa Henrietta of Brandenburg, three by Paul Gerhard, and one by Count Zinzendorf. The one by Luther seems (in the original) to contain, pressed into it, the history of a lifetime, to be the essence of that "Commentary on the Galatians" which contained, as it were, the essence of Luther's life.

Gerhard's hymn on "God's Providential Care" has been selected as giving the key-note to all his hymns and to his life of conflict and victory. The hymn on "Heaven," by Gerhard,[1] is given on account of its deep view of the happiness of heaven, as consisting in seeing the face of God.

And finally, the hymn by Count Zinzendorf has been chosen because (like the previous hymn of Luther's and that on the "Passion," by Paul Gerhard) it traces back our redemption to the deep fountain of the love of the Father, and, while penetrated with the absolute need of an atoning sacrifice, in order that the lost may be saved, dwells on that sacrifice as made by God Himself.

A SONG OF PRAISE FOR THE GREAT BENEFITS WHICH GOD HAS MANIFESTED TO US IN CHRIST.[2]

Evangelischer Liederschatz von Albrecht Knapp, 215.

(*Nun freut euch lieben Christeng'ein.*)

I.

Dear Christian people, all rejoice,
Each soul with joy upspringing;

---

[1] This is translated from a hymn in Albrecht Knapp's collection, said to be "after Gerhard."   [2] Luther's own title.

Pour forth one song with heart and voice,
    With love and gladness singing.
Give thanks to God, our Lord above,
Thanks for His miracle of Love!
        Dearly he hath redeem'd us!

2.

The devil's captive, bound I lay,
    Lay in death's chains forlorn!
My sins distress'd me night and day,
    The sin within me born:
I could not do the thing I would,
In all my life was nothing good,
        Sin had possess'd me wholly.

3.

My good works could no comfort shed,
    Worthless must they be rated;
My free-will to all good was dead,
    And God's just judgments hated.
Me of all hope my sins bereft;
Nothing but death to me was left,
        And death was hell's dark portal.

4.

Then God saw, with deep pity moved,
    My grief that knew no measure;
Pitying He saw, and freely loved,—
    To save me was His pleasure,
The Father's heart to me was stirr'd,
He saved me with no sovereign word,—
        His very best it cost Him.

5.

He spoke to His Beloved Son,
    With infinite compassion:

"Go hence, my heart's most precious crown,
    Be to the lost salvation.
Death, his relentless tyrant, slay,
And bear him from his sins away
        With Thee to live for ever!"

6.

Willing the Son took that behest:
    Born of a maiden mother,
To His own earth He came a guest,
    And made Himself my brother.
All secretly He went His way,
Veil'd in my mortal flesh He lay,
        And thus the Foe He vanquish'd.

7.

He said to me, "Cling close to Me,
    Thy sorrows now are ending;
Freely I give Myself for thee,
    Thy life with Mine defending.
For I am thine and thou art Mine,
And where I am there thou shalt shine,
        The Foe shall never reach us.

8.

"True, he will shed my heart's life-blood,
    And torture me to death;
All this I suffer for thy good,
    This hold with firmest faith.
Death dieth through My life divine:
I, sinless, bear those sins of thine;
        And so shalt thou be rescued.

9.

"I rise again to heaven from hence
    High to My Father soaring,

Thy Master there to be, and thence
  My Spirit on thee pouring:
In every grief to comfort thee,
And teach thee more and more of Me,
    Into all truth still guiding.

10.

"What I have done and taught on earth,
  Do thou, and teach, none dreading;
That so God's kingdom may go forth,
  And His high praise be spreading;
And guard thee from the words of men,
Lest the great joy be lost again:
    This My last charge I leave thee."

THE LAMB OF GOD.

Albrecht Knapp, 444.

BY PAUL GERHARD.

(*Ein Lämmlein geht und trägt die Schuld.*)

1.

A Lamb goes uncomplaining forth,
  The guilt of all men bearing;
Laden with all the sin of earth,
  None else the burden sharing!
Goes patient on, grows weak and faint,
To slaughter led without complaint,
  That spotless life to offer;
Bears shame and stripes, and wounds, and death,
Anguish and mockery, and saith,
  "Willing all this I suffer."

2.

That Lamb is Lord of death and life,
  God over all for ever;

The Father's Son, whom to that strife
   Love doth for us deliver!
O mighty Love! what hast thou done!
The Father offers up His Son,
   The Son content descendeth!
O Love, O Love! how strong art Thou!
In shroud and grave thou lay'st Him low
   Whose word the mountains rendeth!

3.

Him on the Cross, O Love, thou layest,
   Fast to that torture nailing,
Him as a spotless Lamb thou slayest;
   His heart and flesh are failing;
The body with that crimson flood,
That precious tide of noble blood,
   The heart with anguish breaking!
O Lamb! what shall I render Thee
For all Thy tender love to me,
   Or what return be making?

4.

My lifelong days would I still Thee
   Be steadfastly beholding;
Thee ever, as Thou ever me,
   With loving arms infolding.
And when my heart grows faint and chill,
My heart's undying Light, oh still
   Abide unchanged before me!
Myself Thy heritage I sign,
Ransom'd to be for ever thine,
   My only hope and glory.

5.

I of Thy majesty and grace
   Would night and day be singing;

A sacrifice of joy and praise
    Myself to Thee still bringing.
My stream of Life shall flow to Thee,
Its steadfast current ceaselessly
    In praise to Thee outpouring;
And all the good Thou dost to me
I'll treasure in my memory,
    Deep in my heart's depths storing.

6.

Gate of my heart, fly open wide,
    Shrine of my heart, spread forth;
The Treasure will in thee abide,
    Greater than heaven and earth.
Away with all this poor world's treasures,
And all this vain world's tasteless pleasures,
    My treasure is in heaven :
For I have found true riches now;
My treasure, Christ, my Lord art Thou,
    Thy blood so freely given !

7.

This treasure ever I employ,
    This ever aid shall yield me ;
In sorrow it shall be my joy,
    In conflict it shall shield me.
In joy, the music of my feast :
And when all else has lost its zest,
    This manna still shall feed me ;
In thirst my drink, in want my food,
My company in solitude,
    To comfort and to lead me !

8.

Death's poison cannot harm me now,
    Thy blood new life bestowing;

My shadow from the heat art Thou,
  When the noontide is glowing.
And when by inward grief opprest,
My aching heart in Thee shall rest,
  As tired head on pillow.
Should storms of persecution toss,
Firm anchor'd by Thy saving Cross,
  My bark rests on the billow!

9.

And when at last Thou leadest me
  Into Thy joy and light,
Thy blood shall clothe me royally,
  Making my garments white;
Shall place upon my head the crown,
Shall lead me to the Father's throne,
  And raiment fit provide me;
Till I, by Him to Thee betrothed,
By Thee in bridal vesture clothed,
  Stand as a bride beside Thee!

ON THE RESURRECTION OF THE JUST.

Albrecht Knapp, 585.

BY THE ELECTRESS LOUISA HENRIETTA OF BRANDENBURG.

(*Jesus meine Zuversicht.*)

1.

Jesus, my eternal trust,
  And my Saviour, ever liveth:
This I know: and deep and just
  Is the peace this knowledge giveth,
Though death's lingering night may start
Many a question in my heart.

2.

Jesus lives eternally;
   I shall also live in Him,
Where my Saviour is shall be.
   What can make this bright hope dim?
Will the head one member lose,
Nor through each its life diffuse?

3.

Hope's strong chain around me bound,
   Still shall twine my Saviour grasping;
And my hand of faith be found
   As death left it, Jesus clasping:
No assault the foe can make
E'er that deathless clasp shall break!

4.

I am flesh, and therefore duly
   Dust and ashes must become;
This I know, but know as truly
   He will wake me from the tomb,
That with Him, whate'er betide,
I may evermore abide!

5.

God Himself in that blest place
   Shall a glorious body give me
I shall see His blissful face,
   To His heav'ns He will receive me:
To His joyful presence raise,
Ever upon Christ to gaze!

6.

Then these eyes my Lord shall know,
   My Redeemer and my Brother:

In His love my soul shall glow,—
   I myself, and not another!
Then from this rejoicing heart
Every weakness shall depart.

7.

What is weak or maim'd below,
   There shall be made strong and free;
Earthly is the seed we sow,
   Heavenly shall the harvest be:
Nature here, and sin; but there,
Spiritual all and fair!

8.

Thrill, my mortal frame, with gladness,
   Fear not though thy vigour wane,
Give not any place to sadness,
   Die, yet Christ shall raise again,
When shall sound the trump of doom,
Piercing, rending every tomb!

9.

Smile, then, that cold dark grave scorning,
   Smile at death and hell together,
Through the free air of the morning,
   To your Saviour ye shall gather;
All infirmity and woe
'Neath your feet then lying low.

10.

Only raise your souls above
   Pleasures in which earth delighteth;
Give your hearts to Him in love
   To whom death so soon uniteth;
Thither oft in spirit flee
Where ye would for ever be.

ON THE PROVIDENCE OF GOD.

Albrecht Knapp, 125.

BY PAUL GERHARD.

(*Befiehl du deine Wege.*)

Commit thy way to God,
  The load which makes thee faint,
Worlds are to Him no load!—
  To Him breathe thy complaint.
He who for winds and clouds
  Maketh a pathway free,
Through wastes, or hostile crowds,
  Can make a way for thee.

Thou must in Him be blest,
  Ere bliss can be secure;
On His work must thou rest,
  If thy work shall endure.
To anxious, prying thought,
  And weary, fretting care,
The Highest yieldeth nought;
  He giveth all to prayer!

Father! thy faithful love,
  Thy mercy, wise and mild,
Sees what will blessing prove,
  Or what will hurt Thy child.
And what Thy wise foreseeing
  Doth for Thy children choose,
Thou bringest into being,
  Nor sufferest them to lose.

All means always possessing,
  Invincible in might;
Thy doings are all blessing,
  Thy goings are all light.

Nothing Thy work suspending,
  No foe can make Thee pause,
When Thou Thine own defending
  Dost undertake their cause.

Though all the devils throng
  Thine onward course to stay,
Thou passest calm along,
  Nor swervest from Thy way.
What Thou hast once disposed
  And order'd in Thy strength,
Whatever powers opposed,
  Must reach its goal at length.

Hope then, though woes be doubled,
  Hope and be undismay'd;
Let not thine heart be troubled,
  Nor let it be afraid.
This prison where thou art,
  Thy God will break it soon,
And flood with light Thy heart
  In His own blessed noon.

Up, up! the day is breaking,
  Say to thy cares, Good night!
Thy troubles from thee shaking,
  Like dreams in day's fresh light.
Thou wearest not the crown,
  Nor the best course canst tell;
God sitteth on the throne,
  And guideth all things well.

Trust Him to govern, then!
  No king can rule like Him;
How wilt thou wonder when
  Thine eyes no more are dim:

To see these paths which vex thee,
   How wise they were, and meet;
The works which now perplex thee,
   How beautiful, complete!

Faithful the love thou sharest,
   All, all is well with thee;
The crown from hence thou bearest
   With shouts of victory.
In thy right hand, to-morrow,
   Thy God shall place the palms;
To Him who chased thy sorrow
   How glad will be thy psalms!

THE JOYS OF HEAVEN.

Albrecht Knapp, 3045.

AFTER PAUL GERHARD.

(*Ach Jesu, wie so schön.*)

O Christ! how good and fair
Will be my portion, where
Thine eyes on me shall rest,
And make me fully blest,
When from this narrow earth
To Thee I shall spring forth!

What joy, unmix'd and full,
Thou Treasure of the soul,
When, in that home above,
Thy heart speaks out its love
To all made one with Thee,
My brothers, Lord, and me!

What glorious light will shine
Forth from Thy face Divine,

Which, in that life untold,
Then first I shall behold!
How will Thy goodness free
Fill me with ecstasy!

Lips, whence such words have stream'd!
Eyes, whence such pity beam'd!
Side, wounded once for me!
All, all I then shall see!
With reverent rapture greet
Thy piercèd hands and feet!

Ah, Jesus, my "good part!"
How will my mind and heart
Vibrate with rapture through,
And all my soul grow new,
When Thou, with smiles of love,
Openest those gates above!

"Come," Thou wilt say, "blest child!
Taste pleasures undefiled,
And see the gifts, how fair,
My Father's hands prepare;
Pasture thine heart for ever
In joy that fadeth never."

O thou poor, passing earth!
What are thy treasures worth
Beside those heavenly crowns
And more than golden thrones
Which Christ hath treasured there
For those who please Him here!

This is the angels' land,
Where all the blessed stand!
Here I hear nought but singing,
See all with gladness springing;

Here is no cross, no sorrow,
No parting on the morrow!

When shall that joy begin?
When wilt Thou call me in?
Thou knowest; but my feet
Press onward Thee to meet;
And my heart, day by day,
Bears me to Thee away.

ON THE LOVE OF GOD.

Albrecht Knapp, 1136.

COUNT ZINZENDORF.

(*Du ewiger Abgrund der seligen Liebe.*)

Thou deep abyss of blessed Love,
   In Jesus Christ to us unseal'd,
Fire, which no finite heart could prove,
   Depths, to no human thought reveal'd;
Thou lovest sinners, lovest me!
Thou blessest those who cursèd Thee:
O great, O kind, O loving One,
What worthless creatures shin'st Thou on!

Thou King of Light! our deepest longing
   Is shallow to Thy depths of grace;
Deep are the woes to us belonging,
   But deeper far Thy joy to bless.
Teach us to trust the Father's love,
Still looking to the Son above;
Blest Spirit! through our spirits pour
True prayers and praises evermore.

Jesus! Thine own with rich grace filling,
    Thy mighty blessing on us shed,
New life through every member thrilling,
    Diffused from Thee, the living Head;
Show us how light Thy mild yoke is,
And how from self's hard yoke it frees.
If Thou wilt teach Thy household so,
The works the Master's hand shall show.

CHAPTER X

HYMNS OF SWEDEN AND OTHER COUNTRIES

LONG after the southern regions of modern Europe emerge into the sober daylight of history, the twilight of legend lingers over the North. The gigantic forms of the old Sagas flit about in the gleam of the northern lights ages after the chronicles of the South are peopled with a race of solid and ordinary men and women. Four centuries after the times when the people of Milan first sang the hymns of Ambrose, nearly three centuries after Gregory the Great sent Augustine to the English, a hundred years after the Venerable Bede passed his tranquil life in the monastery near Wearmouth, translating the New Testament into Anglo-Saxon, and chronicling his own times, in Sweden Christianity was carrying on its first conflict with the fierce old Scandinavian heathenism.—Anschar, "the Apostle of the North," died A.D. 835.

Thus Christendom had journeyed eight hundred years from the apostolic age before the name of Christ penetrated into Sweden.

The Swedish Reformation seems scarcely to have been so much a transplantation from Germany as a natural branch of Lutheran Protestantism. The inward work in Sweden appears to have followed the outward. The Bible was given to the people in their mother-tongue, and the Church services were reformed on the Lutheran model, and so the nation became Lutheran, and many among them truly evangelical. The Bible was translated from the German Bible; the hymn-book was a reflection of the German hymn-book, but by degrees native hymn-writers arose. The glad tidings could not fail to call forth the new song.

The whole history of Sweden appears to blossom into its full and characteristic development in the biography of one man. It should not be forgotten that the royal hero of Protestantism was a Swede. Swedish chronicles, otherwise so isolated, are incorporated as a central portion of European history around the persons of two Swedish kings, Gustavus Adolphus and Charles XII. The self-sacrificing Christian hero, and the selfish military chief, might stand as among the most strikingly contrasted types of true and false heroism.

If ever a man subordinated self to the cause he contended for, it was surely the great Gustavus. And he had his reward in kind. The life he so unflinchingly offered to stem the returning flood of Romanism was accepted; and the flood was stayed. The hero died at Lützen; and the faith he had contended for held its ground in Germany. From that noble heart, in which northern strength and northern tenderness, the lofty heroism of an old Viking, and the lowly heroism of a Christian martyr, were so wonderfully blended, one psalm has come down to us. Its composition was characteristic. The brave king was no man of letters. The fire of faith which burned in his heart was more wont to fuse the iron of heroic deeds than the gold of beautiful words. But the thoughts were in his heart; had they not inspired him in march and battle-field? So he told his chaplain, Dr. Jacob Fabricius, what his thoughts were, and the chaplain moulded them into three verses of a hymn, and the simple-hearted hero took them ever afterwards as his battle-song. On the morning of his last battle, when the armies of Gustavus and Wallenstein were drawn up, waiting till the morning mist dispersed to commence the attack, the king commanded Luther's grand psalm, "Eine feste Burg ist unser Gott!" to be sung, and then that hymn of his own, accompanied by the drums and trumpets of the whole army. Immediately afterwards the mist broke, and the sunshine burst on the two armies. For a moment Gustavus Adolphus knelt beside his horse, in face of his soldiers, and repeated his usual battle-prayer, "O Lord Jesus Christ! bless our arms, and this day's battle, for the glory of Thy holy name!" Then passing along the lines, with a few brief words of encouragement, he gave the battle-cry, "God with us!" the same with which he had conquered at Leipzig. Thus began the day which laid him low amidst the thickest of the fight, with those three sentences on his dying lips, noble and Christian as any that ever fell from the lips of dying man since the days of the first martyr: "I seal with my blood the liberty and religion of the German nation!"—"My God, my God!"—and the last that were heard, "Alas! my poor queen!"[1]

A hymn so consecrated has a value beyond that of any mere words. Whether the Swedish (from which the following translation is made) or the German was the original, the translator does not know. Probably both were original; but that in the mother-tongue of the hero himself has its peculiar interest.

GUSTAVUS ADOLPHUS' BATTLE-SONG.

(*Förfäras ej du lilla hop.*)

Be not dismay'd, thou little flock,
Although the foe's fierce battle shock
    Loud on all sides assail thee.
Though o'er thy fall they laugh secure,
Their triumph cannot long endure;
    Let not thy courage fail thee.

Thy cause is God's; go at His call,
And to His hand commit thy all;
    Fear thou no ill impending:
His Gideon shall arise for thee,
God's Word and people manfully,
    In God's own time, defending.

Our hope is sure in Jesus' might;
Against themselves the godless fight,
    Themselves, not us, distressing;
Shame and contempt their lot shall be;
God is with us, with Him are we:
    To us belongs His blessing.

[1] Hollings' "Life of Gustavus Adolphus."

The orphaned army and nation had need, indeed, of such words to sustain them for the loss of such a man and such a captain; a loss inadequately compensated even by the utter destruction on that battle-field of the imperial army. But his cause was won, and Protestant Germany was saved, not by her armies or her princes, but by the heart of that one hero, given by God.

Two other translations are here offered from Swedish hymns. The first is from one by Spegel, Archbishop of Upsala. He was born A.D. 1645, thirteen years after the death of the great Gustavus, and died A.D. 1714; he was thus a contemporary of Paul Gerhard. He is said by his countrymen to be their greatest hymn-writer, and to have accomplished much good for Sweden. The following verses are extracted from a hymn of his, which is a paraphrase of part of the Sermon on the Mount.

"CONSIDER THE LILIES."

(Oss Christna bör tro och besinna.)

We, Christians, should steadfastly ponder
  What Christ hath so graciously taught;
For He, who would have us His freemen,
  Would see us retain in our thought
How little things earthly are worth,
Lest those who heap treasures on earth
  The heavenly prize leave unsought.

All nature a sermon may preach thee;
  The birds sing thy murmurs away,—
The birds which, nor sowing nor reaping,
  God fails not to feed day by day;

And He, who these creatures doth cherish,
Will He fail thee and leave thee to perish?
　Or art thou not better than they?

The lilies, nor toiling nor spinning,
　Their clothing how gorgeous and fair!
What tints in their tiny robes woven,
　What wondrous devices are there!
All Solomon's stores could not render
One festival robe of such splendour
　As the flowers have for everyday wear.

God gives to each flower its rich raiment,
　And o'er them His treasures flings free,
Which to-day finds so fragrant in beauty,
　And to-morrow all faded shall see.
Thus the lilies smile shame on thy care,
And the happy birds sing it to air:
　Will their God be forgetful of thee!

The last of these three specimens of Swedish sacred song is from Franzén, Bishop of Hernösand, who died A.D. 1818, at the age of thirty-six.

LOOKING UNTO JESUS.

FRANZÉN.

(*Jesum haf i ständigt minne.*)

Jesus in thy memory keep,
　Would'st thou be God's child and friend;
Jesus in thy heart shrined deep,
　Still thy gaze on Jesus bend.
In thy toiling, in thy resting,
Look to Him with every breath,
Look to Jesus' life and death.

Look to Jesus, till, reviving,
   Faith and love thy life-springs swell;
Strength for all things good deriving
   From Him who did all things well;
Work, as He did, in thy season,
Works which shall not fade away,
Work while it is called to-day.

Look to Jesus, prayerful, waking,
   When thy feet on roses tread;
Follow, worldly pomp forsaking,
   With thy cross, where He hath led.
Look to Jesus in temptation;
Baffled shall the Tempter flee,
And God's angels come to thee.

Look to Jesus when dark lowering
   Perils thy horizon dim,
By that band in terror cowering,
   Calm 'midst tempests, look on Him.
Trust in Him who still rebuketh
Wind and billow, fire and flood;
Forward! brave by trusting God.

Look to Jesus when distressed,
   See what He, the Holy, bore;
Is thy heart with conflict pressed;
   Is thy soul still harass'd sore?
See His sweat of blood, His conflict,
Watch His agony increase,
Hear His prayer, and feel His peace.

By want's fretting thorns surrounded,
   Does long pain press forth thy sighs?
By ingratitude deep wounded,
   Does a scornful world despise?

Friends forsake thee, or deny thee?
See what Jesus must endure,
He who as the light was pure!

Look to Jesus still to shield thee
  When no longer thou mayest live;
In that last need He will yield thee
  Peace the world can never give.
Look to Him, thy head low bending;
He who finish'd all for thee,
Takes thee, then, with Him to be.

Were it within the scope of this volume to give selections from living hymn-writers, many might be chosen from Sweden, where a fresh glow of Christian life is, in these days, awakening many a fresh stream of song in a language which combines the homely strength of the German with the liquid music of the Italian.

One French and two Italian hymns are added as an instance of the unity of the voice of Christian life in modern days. One of them is by a famous poet; the other two are simple popular hymns, authors unknown.

AMOUR DE DIEU.

A children's hymn sung in a country church.

De tous les biens que tu nous donnes
Le seul que doive nous charmer,
Ce n'est ni l'or ni les couronnes,
Mon Dieu, c'est le don de t'aimer.

A ses attraits c'est faire outrage
Que de vouloir se partager ;
C'est donc à toi que je m'engage
Aujourd'hui pour ne plus changer.
De tous, etc.

Dans cet exil rien n'est durable
Et tout y doit finir son cours ;
Dieu seul est à jamais aimable,
C'est lui que j'aimerai toujours.
De tous, etc.

Auteur souverain de mon être !
À qui dois-je le consacrer,
Sinon au Dieu qui me fit naître
Pour le servir et l'adorer ?
De tous, etc.

Dieu de mon cœur, oui, je l'atteste,
Dès ce jour j'embrasse ta loi ;
À tes pieds je jure et proteste
De ne plus vivre que pour toi.
De tous, etc.

LA PENTECOSTE.

BY MANZONI.

Madre dei Santi, immagine
  Della Città superna,
  Del sangue incorruttibile
  Conservatrice eterna ;
  Tu, che da tanti secoli
  Soffri, combatti, e preghi ;
  Che le tue tende spieghi
  Dall' uno all' altro mar ;

Campo di quei, che sperano,
  Chiesa del Dio vivente,
  Dov'éri mai ? qual angolo
  Ti raccoglica nascente,
  Quando il tuo Rè, dai perfidi
  Tratto a morir sul colle,
  Imporporò le zolle
  Dal suo sublime altar ?

E allor, che delle tenebre
  La diva spoglia uscita,
  Mise il potente anelito
  Della seconda vita ;
  E quando in man recandosi
  Il prezzo del perdono,
  Da questa polve al trono
  Del Genitor salì ;

Compagni del suo gemito,
  Conscia de' suoi misteri,
  Tu, della sua vittoria
  Figlia immortal, dov'eri ?
  Tu tuo terror sol vigile,
  Sol nell' obblio secura,
  Stavi in reposte mura,
  Fino a quel sacro dì,

Quando su te lo Spirito
  Rinnovator discese,
  E l' inconsunta fiaccola
  Nella tua destra accese ;
  Quando segnal dei popoli
  Ti collocò sul monte ;
  E ne' tuoi labbri il fonte
  Della parola aprì.

Come la luce rapida
   Piove di cosa in cosa,
   E i colori varii suscita,
   Ovunque si reposa ;
   Tal risonò moltiplice
   La voce dello Spiro :
   L'Arabo, il Parto, il Siro
   In suo sermon l'udì.

Nova franchigia annunziano
   I cieli, e genti nove ;
   Nove, conquiste, e gloria
   Vinta in più belle prove ;
   Nova, ai terrori immobile,
   E alle lusinghe infide,
   Pace, che il mondo irride,
   Ma che rapir non può.

Oh Spirto ! supplichevoli
   A' tuoi solenni altari,
   Soli per selve inospite,
   Vaghi in deserti mari,
   Dall' Ande algenti al Libano
   D'Ibernia all' irta Haiti,
   Sparsi per tutti i liti,
   Ma d'un cor solo in Te,

Noi t'imploriam : placabile
   Spirto discendi ancora
   Ai tuoi cultor propizio,
   Propizio a che t'ignora ;
   Scendi e ricrea : rianima
   I cor nel dubbio estinti;
   E sia divina ai vinti
   Il vincitor mercè.

Discendi, Amor; negli animi
  L'ire superbe attuta:
  Dona i pensier, che il memore
  Ultimo dì non muta:
  Idoni tuoi benefica
  Nutra la tua virtude:
  Siccome il sol, che schiude
  Dal pigro germe il fior:

Che lento poi su le umili
  Erbe morrà non colto,
  Ne sorgerà coi fulgidi
  Color del lembo sciolto,
  Se fuso a lui nell' etere
  Non tornerà quel mite
  Lume, dator di vite,
  E infaticato altor.

Spira dei nostri bamboli
  Nell' innocente riso;
  Spargi la casta porpora
  Alle donzelle in viso;
  Manda alle ascose vergini
  Le pure gioje ascose
  Consacra delle spose
  Il verecondo amor.

Tempra dei baldi giovani
  Il confidente ingegno;
  Reggi il viril proposito
  Ad infallibil segno;
  Adorna la canizie
  Di liete voglie sante;
  Brilla nel guardo errante
  Di chi sperando muor.

LA CROCE.

A popular Song of N. Italy.

Quando nacqui mi disse una voce,
"Tu sei nato a portar la tua croce."
Io piangendo la croce abbracciai
   Che assegnata dal cielo mi fu :
Poi guardai, guardai, guardai,
   Tutti portan la croce quaggiù.

Vidi un Rè tra Baroni e scudieri
Sotto il peso di cupi pensieri,
E al valetto che stava alla porta
   Domandai "Cosa pensa il tuo Rè ?"
Mi rispose "alla croce egli pensa
   Che col trono il Signore gli diè."

Vidi un giorno tornare un soldato
Dalla guerra col braccio troncato,
"Perche piangi," gli dissi, "o fratello,
   Non ti basta la croce d'onor ?"
Mi rispose "passaro, bei giorni
   Altra croce mi ha data il Signor."

Vidi un uomo giulivo nel volto.
In mantello di seta envolto
"Par te solo," gli dissi, "o fratello
   E la vita cosparsa di fior ?"
Non rispose ma asperse il mantello ;—
   La sua croce l'aveva sul cuor

Più e più allora abbracciai la fatica,
Ch'è la croce dei poveri amica ;
E di pianto tallor la bagniai
   Ne la voglio lasciare mai più !
O fratelli ; guardai, guardai,
   Tutti portan la croce quaggiù !

CHAPTER XI

ENGLISH HYMNS

THE Reformed Churches of France and French Switzerland seem to have had no literature corresponding to the hymns of Protestant Germany. The names connected with mediæval hymn literature, on the other hand, are, as has been observed, chiefly French. Did the peculiar form which the Reformation took in France, then, tend to quench the spirit of sacred poetry, or what other causes brought about this result?

To judge rightly on this subject, we must, in the first place, be clear what we mean by France, since, although the French monarchy is the oldest in Europe, the same antiquity can scarcely be assigned to the French nation as it now exists. The distracted aggregation of duchies and counties, Brittany, Burgundy, Aquitaine, Provence, Languedoc, out of which the unity of modern France was gradually compressed, was scarcely more one with the France of to-day than the Greece of Marathon was with the Byzantine Empire. The southern regions were of the South, Romance, the northern were of the North, Teutonic, and neither were French. It is remarkable how many of the names of the mediæval hymn-writers, connected by birth with France, are of German form. Bernard, with his brother Gerard, Marbod, Hildebert, seem more the natural predecessors of Martin Luther and Paul Gerhard than of Corneille or Clement Marot. Lineally, therefore, the German hymn literature may be said to be descended from the mediæval; and the sacred Latin poetry, which seemed native to France, may perhaps rather be looked on as a branch of the great river of German sacred song.

Yet when we remember that a similar absence of an evangelical national hymn literature, springing up spontaneously as a natural growth of the Reformation, which characterizes the Reformed Churches of France and French Switzerland, exists also in the kindred Church of Scotland, it is impossible not to connect this fact with the similar form which the Reformation took in all these lands. None of the strictly Calvinistic communities have a hymn-book dating back to the Reformation. It cannot surely be their doctrine which caused this; many of the best known and most deeply treasured of the more modern hymns of Germany and England have been written by those who received the doctrines known as Calvinistic. Nor can it proceed from any peculiarity of race, or deficiency in popular love of music and song. French and Scotch national character are too dissimilar to explain the resemblance; whilst France has many national melodies and songs, and Scotland is peculiarly rich in both. Is not the cause then simply the common ideal of external ecclesiastical forms which pervaded all the Churches reformed on the Genevan type? The intervening chapters of ecclesiastical history were, as it were, folded up, as too blotted and marred for truth to be read to profit in them; and, next to the first chapter of Church History in the Acts of the Apostles, was to stand, as the second chapter, the history of the Reformed Churches. Words were to resume their original Bible meaning; nothing was to be received that could not be traced back to the Divine hand. Ecclesiastical order was to be such as St. Paul had established, or had found established; clearly to be traced, it was believed, in the Acts and Apostolical Epistles. And since the inspiration which glowed on the gifted lips of apostolic days existed no longer, and the psalms and hymns and spiritual songs in which St. Paul had delighted formed no part of the New Testament canon, recourse must be had to an older liturgy, inspired throughout, at once most human and most Divine. Thus the Book of Psalms became the hymn-book of the Reformed Churches, adapted to grave and solemn music, in metrical translations whose one·aim and glory was to render into measure which could be sung the very words of the old Hebrew Psalms. By what ingenious transpositions and compressions of words and syllables this has been accomplished, in the case of Scotland, is known to those who attend the Scotch Presbyterian services. The labour must have been conscientiously and painfully accomplished; for although the result may, to the uninitiated, bear something of the same resemblance to poetry as the fitting of fragments of Hebrew temple and Christian church into the walls of Jerusalem bears to architecture,—columns reversed and mouldings disconnected,—yet the very words are certainly there, and the use to which they are applied is most sacred. At all events, the Scotch Psalms are David's Psalms, and not modern meditations on them; and with all the sacred associations which two centuries of such a Church history as that of Scotland has gathered round the song of to-day, mingling it with echoes from mountain-gatherings, and martyrs' prisons and scaffolds, and joyful deathbeds, probably no hymn-book could ever be one-half so musical or poetical to Scotch hearts as those strange, rough verses. The Paraphrases combined with them, which for the last hundred years have been the hymn-book of the Scottish people, have a later origin and another history, and do not alter the fact that David's Psalter was the first hymn-book of the Reformed or Genevan Churches.

England, in this as in so many other things, takes a middle place;—in some measure a city of refuge, where both forms of the Reformation lived tranquilly side by side, but also a border-land, where both met and contended.

The Church of England is, in form, linked to the Mediæval Church by ties far stronger and more numerous than the Lutheran Churches of Germany. The thinking people of England were, after the Marian exiles returned from the Continent, more strongly attracted to the Protestantism of Switzerland and Scotland than to that of Germany. Thus, between Anglicanism and Puritanism it happened that, until the last century, we cannot be said to have had any national—that is, any people's hymn-book at all. Probably no person or community ever felt any enthusiasm either for Sternhold and Hopkins or Tate and Brady; and although some stray hymns had crept into our modern hymn-books from earlier days, until the eighteenth century we had no People's Hymn-book; none, that is, that was placed on cottage tables beside the Bible, and sung when Christians met, and chanted beside the grave. The Wesleys seem to have been the first who gave a People's Hymn-book to England; unless that of Dr. Watts may be called so, published about the beginning of the eighteenth century. Not, indeed, that England was silent those two hundred years, or that the sacred chain of holy song was ever altogether broken in our country. We had our "Te Deum" and "Magnificat," and the English Psalms in the music of their grand and touching prose; a melody as much deeper to our ears than any metrical manufacture of the same, as the morning song of a thrush is deeper than the notes of a caged bird that has been painfully taught to sing two or three tunes. These were said in village church and quiet home, making rich melody in the heart, and pealed through the old cathedrals to choral chant in a language "understanded of all the people." The Prayer-book, with all its musical flow of choice words floating down on its clear stream of pure English the song and prayer of the true Church of all ages, and the English Psalter,— this was the hymn-book of half our people; while in many a Puritan congregation the heroic purposes of the heart, the individuality of Puritan religion, which made every hymn sung as by each worshipper alone " to God," must have breathed poetry into any verses, and fused them by inward fire, into a music no external polish could ever give.

Many a solitary voice also poured its quiet lay apart, enough to make a joyous chorus to those heavenly listeners who could hear all together. Still there was no People's Hymn-book; no hymns which the babe could lisp and the dying rejoice in, linking together, by the power of simple truth, the cradle and the deathbed. The language of sacred poetry in Queen Elizabeth's time was too subtle and fanciful ever to come home to the hearts of the people. In spirit evangelical, in form they were like the Latin verses of later mediæval hymn-writers, written for a choice few to enjoy, and full of those subtle allusions, half the pleasure of which consists in the ingenuity required to understand as well as to invent them. Such hymns could never be sung, like Luther's, by little children at Christmas, or become a nation's battle-song, or sweetly distil peace at moments when flesh and heart failed, and mental effort was impossible, clinging around the soul, as it were, by their own simple power, when the soul had lost its power to cling to anything. At such times, the minds which framed them must surely have fallen thankfully back on the old psalms and scriptural hymns, however rough the setting. These ingenious poems have become obsolete, which deeper things cannot. The fashion of this world was on them, and they have passed away. Whilst the name of Luther is even to us in England a household name and the hymns of the earliest Reformers are reprinted fresh as at first in the latest German hymn-books, how many among us know anything of the names of Gascoigne, Barnaby Barnes, Michael Drayton, Henry Lok, William Hunnis, or Samuel Rowlands, who wrote sacred poems in the days of Good Queen Bess? Edmund Spenser and Sir Philip Sidney are, indeed, familiar names; but although fragments of Spenser's high and sweet meditations may find their way into a collection of sacred poems, they are scarcely hymns for general use; and although Sir Philip Sidney and Lady Pembroke's Psalter contains many majestic and vigorous versions, it was never a people's Psalter. The rich old English, and the deep thought and quaint fancies of that wonderful period, shine out in many of those forgotten pages; but they bear witness to the piety or the poetical power of the writer rather than to the faith of the times. Taken, however, as they are, they have their deep interest. If not echoed back, like the hymns of Luther and Gerhard, by the hearts of thousands, they are at least parts in the great service of song, which has its sweet solitary hymns, sung on through the night as well as its grand choral bursts at morning.

At last the strong hand of Queen Elizabeth lay powerless; and through the reigns of the Stuarts England passed on to the Rebellion, and the firm rule of Oliver Cromwell. The reign of "euphuism" died out: sacred music must cast aside the fair trappings of the golden age, and lay down the lyre, and chant strains preluded by trumpets, interrupted by cannon, and often echoed from prisons and scaffolds. All the contrary elements in the English Church and State, which in their passive condition neutralized each other, sprang into activity; every difference became a dispute; the electricity which in calm weather quickened life, exploded in thunderstorms. Yet from both sides, amidst the din, the old psalm flowed on piercing with its music all the clamour, and reaching us long after the echoes of the storm have died away. George Herbert, from his country parsonage ministering to the poor, and borne to his grave with cathedral chants; blind John Milton, Secretary of the Protector, and scorn of the court of the Restoration; Richard Baxter, true pastor of the flock of Christ at Kidderminster, so basely browbeaten by Judge Jeffreys; Bishop Ken, the Nonjuror; these are the voices which carry on the song of peace through that time of strife.

With the eighteenth century, however, the history of English hymn-books must begin. The two earliest names on the long list of that century link the story of the faith in England, in an interesting way, with that of the persecuted Protestants on the Continent. Dr. Watts, born in 1674, was descended, through his mother, from a Huguenot family, driven from France by the persecutions in the early part of Queen Elizabeth's reign. And Dr. Doddridge, doubtless, in his childhood, when his mother had finished the Bible-lesson from the pictured Dutch tiles, would often ask for the story of her father Dr. John Baumann's flight from Bohemia, with his little store of money bound up in his girdle, and Luther's German Bible for all his heritage. Traditions of other ancestral wrongs and faithfulness deepened the early piety of the two great Nonconformist hymn-writers; the pathetic stories of those patient sufferings for conscience' sake, which, next to the martyrdoms of Mary's time, form the most thrilling chapter in the history of English Protestantism,—stories not then condensed into national history, but which the sufferers themselves yet lived to tell: for Dr. Watts' mother also had her tales of her son's own infancy, when his father lay in prison for his convictions, and she had sate on the stones by his prison door with her first-born in her arms. There had been other reasons besides the dearth of writers why the Puritan congregations could have no hymn-books. They had to choose their places of meeting in secluded corners, to set watches outside the door, and let their prayers and praises be soft, so that no enemy might hear and betray them. The times changed much during the lifetime of those two men. The Stuarts were finally dethroned. Dissenting academies began to flourish; and the heroic age of Nonconformity passed away. When at length Dr. Watts died, in a tranquil old age, at Abney Park, in 1748, and was buried among many of his persecuted friends and predecessors in Bunhill Fields, a respectful concourse of spectators attended the funeral. And Dr. Doddridge, when, at fifty-one, consumption had laid him low, on his death-bed on a foreign shore, where only his wife was with him, ministering to him to the last, was followed by the sympathy of good men of all ecclesiastical parties in his native land. It is interesting to know, that Dr. Watts' hymn-book, which the dying Dr. Doddridge found in a friend's house at Lisbon, was often the solace of his last days of suffering.

The lives of these two singers were alike in their calm and sunny peacefulness. Dr. Watts lived without care under the hospitable roof of Sir Thomas Abney, combining the tranquillity of the life of a hermit with the cheerfulness of a social circle. Dr. Doddridge lived surrounded by his affectionate family, and amidst his pupils, in a comfortable old English county-town house at Northampton. Both seemed to have learned, from the traditions of persecution in their families, what persecution teaches few, to forbear. They did what good they could in their own circles, and wrote hymns, which English Christians unite in singing; and which, although many of them may be unworthy of others, and the best may be defective in literary finish, yet fulfil the great mission of hymns, being lisped by infancy and murmured on the deathbed, and welcome alike in the cottage and the palace, wherever sorrow melts men to prayer, or Christian joy awakens them to praise.

And among the foretastes of better things, and the illustration of the true essential unity of all the living Church of Christ, not one of the least satisfactory is the quiet combination, at the end of many of our Prayer-books, of the hymns of the Nonjuring Bishop Ken and the Nonconformist Dr. Doddridge. There is certainly no small pleasure in beholding all the various sections within the Church of England unconsciously unite in praising God in strains which first flowed from minds too far apart at either extreme of her ample enclosure to be included within it. If it is true, as is reported, that Bishop Ken said it would enhance his joy in heaven to listen to his Morning and Evening Hymns sung by the faithful on earth, we may be sure that pleasure would not be marred by hearing blended with them, as the "fair white cloth" is spread, and the worshippers prepare to celebrate the "exceeding great love of our Master and only Saviour Jesus Christ," the hymn of the Nonconformist minister—

"My God, and is Thy table spread,
And doth Thy cup with love o'erflow?"

Serenely, through peaceful times, did these two good men, Doddridge and Watts, pass along their tranquil course to their quiet end, evermore to

"Bathe the weary soul
In seas of heavenly rest."

Less tranquil days followed, and very different was the complexion of the lives of the writers of the next great English People's Hymn-book.

In the first years of the century, whilst Dr. Doddridge, during his solitary childhood, was learning from his mother's lips, in their house in London, how the God who led Israel through the wilderness rescued his exiled grandfather from Bohemia; whilst the first edition of Dr. Watts' Hymn-book was being eagerly bought up in a single year, John and Charles Wesley were spending their childhood in the country parsonage at Epworth in Lincolnshire.[1] The old Puritan blood ran also in their veins; their father's grandfather and father had both been ejected ministers, his father many times in prison on account of his Nonconformity. Their mother's father, Dr. Annesley, was also one of the original Nonconformists, a man of whom his daughter said, that for forty years his deep sense of peace with God through Christ had never been broken, and who died murmuring such words as these, "When I awake up in Thy likeness, I shall be satisfied—satisfied!" But their own early leanings were to the opposite of Dissent. They looked to Thomas à Kempis as a guide, rather than to the Puritan divines. It was not until after years of painful toilings to reach and please God, that the Wesleys became as little children, and learned that God had first loved them, had redeemed them by the blood of His Son, and freely accepted them in Him. But when they were taught this liberating truth of present pardon and adoption, and found that the Shepherd of the sheep is also the Door of the fold, and came straight to Him, and proved that the Sun of the heavenly city is also the Sun of the believing soul, their hearts could not contain the joy. The peace

---

[1] John Wesley was born in 1703, Dr. Doddridge in 1702, and the first edition of Dr. Watts' Hymns appeared and was sold in 1709.

of God came to them, not as a quiet blessedness, unconsciously flowing into their hearts through a mother's lips, but as an overwhelming joy, setting them free from a hard bondage. It was to them no hereditary possession, which they were thankful to be allowed to enjoy in tranquillity, and which they would gladly share with any who wished and asked for it; it was news, good news direct from heaven, glad tidings of great joy for all, which all must know. And through the length and breadth of England and Ireland, across the Atlantic to America, the brothers went up and down for half a century to tell it. They were pelted, threatened, mocked, defamed. They were called Jesuits, Jacobites, blasphemers, and fanatics. Houses in which they rested were besieged and unroofed. They were driven from a Church dearer to them than anything but the souls of men; one of the most orderly and methodical of human beings was forced into the life of an itinerant preacher. But the good news spread: riots spread it, persecution proclaimed it. The death-sleep into which Churchmen and Dissenters alike were falling, was broken; the hearts of thousands were awakened; and the morning hymn of rejoicing multitudes went up to that Sun of righteousness which had arisen with healing in His wings. In one place, where an enraged crowd had rushed into the house where John Wesley was resting, he addressed them with such affectionate faithfulness (appealing to the "thirst" which lay deep in their hearts below their opposition), that the disorderly mob became a peaceable congregation, and tears of penitence streamed over the faces of the ringleaders. At another time, the magistrate who came to prevent Charles Wesley from preaching, was himself arrested by the preacher's words, listened to the end, and went away with a humbled and softened heart. In almost every place where they were thus assailed, societies of true converts sprang up, out of the very ranks of the persecutors. It was out of lives such as these that the Wesleyan Hymn-book was distilled. One hymn was composed after a wonderful escape from an infuriated mob; another after a deliverance from a storm at sea; and all in the intervals of a life of incessant toil. The pressure of trial, and the force of faith, drew many a vigorous hymn from John Wesley; but it was Charles Wesley who, in his prime, on his preaching tours, by the roadside, amidst hostile mobs or devout congregations, and in his old age, in his quiet journeyings from friend to friend, poured forth the great mass of the Wesleyan hymns. When his life of beneficence and courageous conflict was almost over, it must have been a sight to call forth tears, as well as smiles, to see the old gentleman (dressed in winter costume even in the height of summer) dismount from his old grey pony, and leaving it in the little garden before his friend's house in the City Road, enter the parlour, card in hand, and note down the words of some sacred song which had been chiming through his heart.

Those hymns are sung now in collieries and coppermines. How many has their heavenly music strengthened to meet death in the dark coal-pit;

on how many dying hearts have they come back, as from a mother's lips, on the battle-field; beside how many deathbeds have they been chanted by trembling voices, and listened to with joy unspeakable; how many have they supplied with prayer and praise, from the first thrill of spiritual fear to the last rapture of heavenly hope! They echo along the Cornish moors as the corpse of the Christian miner is borne to his last resting-place; they cheer with heavenly messages the hard bondage of slavery; they have been the first words of thanksgiving on the lips of the liberated negro; they have given courage to brave men, and patience to suffering women; they have been a liturgy engraven on the hearts of the poor; they have borne the name of Jesus far and wide, and have helped to write it deep on countless hearts. And England is no more without a People's Hymn-book.

But all this time, whilst the Wesleys and Whitefield were evangelizing far and wide, other instruments for the great choral service were being moulded elsewhere.

From the gentle but tortured spirit of Cowper, the glad tidings of grace and redemption drew, in the intervals of his terrible malady, those trembling but immortal notes of praise which are more pathetic than any complainings; for often when he was weeping those touching words on the very bosom of the Father, it seemed to him as if they were echoing unheard through the wastes of the far country.

"O poets! from a maniac's tongue was pour'd the deathless singing;
O Christians! to your cross of hope a hopeless hand is clinging;
O men! this man, in brotherhood your weary paths beguiling,
Groan'd inly while he taught you peace, and died while ye were smiling."[1]

And meanwhile, John Newton, mate of the slaver, guarded, amidst all his sins, from worse, by the recollection of a pious mother, and that pure early attachment to Miss Catlett (afterwards his wife), and at length brought back from his wanderings, to God and home, was receiving his training. He was no man of genius, no born poet like Cowper; yet his hymns are no mere rhymed sermons. He was made a hymn-writer by the depth and freshness of his religious feelings; even as youth or passionate emotion can waken music in many hearts whose ordinary language is a sober colourless prose. His common speech was raised into song by the glory of the message he had to tell, and his own joy in telling it.

Thus, between these two natures, in themselves so diverse, was composed, in the eight years from 1771 to 1779, the "Olney Hymn-book;" a river which welled from very deep sources, and broke through many an adamantine barrier to "make glad the city of God."

The hymn, "God moves in a mysterious way," came into Cowper's heart during a solitary walk in

[1] Elizabeth Barrett-Browning.

the fields, when he was tortured by an apprehension of returning madness. It was the last he ever composed for the Olney collection. The words which have cheered and strengthened so many were wrung from an agonized heart. The veil was not withdrawn from his spirit on earth; but long, long since, wakening up from his "life's long fever" to feel "those eyes" of Infinite Love resting on him, he has learned the blessed meaning of his own words,—

"God is His own interpreter,
And He will make it plain."

Countless other voices followed these, swelling the one chorus of praise. They were not, indeed, always consciously united on earth. It is only in later hymn-books that the names of the Wesleys and Toplady are united; and those who, living, contended in very fierce controversy, being dead, now speak with one accord in two of our most treasured hymns, "Rock of Ages,"[1] and "Jesus, lover of my soul."[2]

And so that generation passed away to learn the full meaning of the words they had been singing, and left to England a rich heritage of sacred song, simple and homely, yet deep as truth, to blend with the earlier psalms which had descended to us from the olden time.

It seems useless to give extracts from hymn-books which are within the reach of every one; but a few specimens from earlier and less accessible writers may be interesting, as a close to this brief sketch of English hymn literature.

[1] Toplady.   [2] Charles Wesley.

POETS OF QUEEN ELIZABETH'S TIME.
THE HIGHWAY TO MOUNT CALUARIE.
SAMUEL ROWLANDS.

Repair to Pilat's hall,
Which place when thou hast found,
There shalt thou see a pillar stand,
To which thy Lord was bound.

'Tis easie to be known
To anie Christian eye;
The bloudie whips doe point it out
From all that stand thereby.

By it there lies a robe
Of purple, and a reed,
Which Pilat's seruants vs'd t' abuse,
In sinne's deriding deed;

When they pronounced "All haile!
God saue thee!" with a breath,
And by the same cride presently,
"Let Christ be done to death."

His person had in scorne,
His doctrine made a iest,
Their mockeries were a martirdome;
No wrongs but Him opprest.

What courage lesse than His
Would haue indur'd like shame,
But would with griefs of such contempt
Haue dide t' indure the same?

A little from that place,
Vpon the left-hand side,
There is a curious portlie dore,
Right beautifull and wide.

Leaue that in anie wise,
Forbid thy foot goe thether;
For out thereat did Judas goe,
Despaire and he together.

But to the right hand turne,
Where is a narrow gate,
Forth which St. Peter went to weepe
His poor distrest estate.

Doe immitate the like,
Goe out at sorrowe's dore;
Weepe bitterly as he did weepe,
That wept to sinne no more.

Keepe wide of Cayphas' house,
Though couetous thoughts infence:
There bribery haunts, despare was hatcht,
False Judas came from thence.

But goe on forward still,
Where Pilat's pallace stands,
There where he first did false condemne,
Then wash his guiltie hands;

Confess'd he found no cause,
And yet condemn'd to die,
Fearing an earthly Caesar more
Than God that rules on hie.

By this direction then,
The way is vnderstood;
No porch, no dore, nor hal to passe,
Vnsprinkled with Christ's blood.

So shall no errour put
Misguiding steppes between;
For euery drop sweet Jesus shed
Is freshly to be seene.

A crowne of piercing thornes
There lies imbru'd in gore;
The garland that thy Sauiour's head
For thy offences wore.

Which when thou shalt behold,
Thinke what His loue hath binne,
Whose head was loaden with those briars
T' vnlade thee of thy sinne;

Whose sacred flesh was torne;
Whose holie skinne was rent;
Whose tortures and extreamest paines
Thy paines in hell preuent.

As God from Babilon
Did turne, when they, past cure,
Refused helpe, whom He would heale,
Denying health t' indure:

So from Hierusalem
The soule's Phisition goes,
When they forsook His sauing health,
And vow'd themselues His foes.

Goe with Him, happie soule,
From that forsaken towne,
Vpon whose wals lies not a stone
But ruin must throw downe.

Followe His feet that goes
For to redeeme thy losse,
And carries all our sinnes with Him
To cansel on His crosse.

Behold what multitudes
Doe guard thy God about,
Who bleeding beares His dying tree
Amidst the Jewish rout!

Looke on with liquid eies,
And sigh from sorrowing mind,
To see the death's-man goe before,
The murdering troupes behind;

Centurion hard at hand,
The thieues upon the side,
The exclamations, shouts, and cries,
The shame He doth abide.

Then presse amongst the throng,
Thyselfe with sorrowes weed;
Get very neare to Christ, and see
What teares the women shed;

Teares that did turne him backe,
They were of such a force,
Teares that did purchase daughters' names
Of Father's kind remorse.

To whom he said, Weepe not;
For me drop not a teare:
Bewaile your offspring, and yourselues,
Griefe's cause vnseen is neare.

Follow their steps in teares,
And with those women mourne,
But not for Christ; weepe for thyselfe,
And Christ will grace returne.

To Pilat's bold demands
He yeelded no replie;
Although the iudge importun'd much
Yet silence did denie.

Vnto his manie words
No answer Christ would make;
Yet to those women did He speake,
For teares' and weepings' sake.

Thinke on their force by teares,
Teares that obtained loue;
Where words too weak could not persuade,
How teares had pouer to moue.

Then looke towards Jesus' load,
More then He could indure,
And how for helpe to beare the same,
A hireling they procure.

Joine thou vnto the crosse;
Bear it of loue's desire,
Doe not as Cyranæus did,
That took it vp for hire.

It is a gratefull deed,
If willing vnderta'ne;
But if compulsion set aworke,
The labour's done in vaine.

The voluntarie death,
That Christ did die for thee,
Giues life to none but such as ioy
Crosse-bearing friends to be.

Vp to Mount Caluerie
If thou desire to goe,
Then take thy crosse and follow Christ,
Thou can'st not misse it so.

When there thou art arriu'd,
His glorious wounds to see,
Say but as faithful as the theife,
O Lord, remember me.

Assure thyselfe to have
A gift all gifts excelling,
Once sold by sinne, once bought by Christ,
For saints' eternall dwelling.

By Adam Paradise
Was sinne's polluted shade;
By Christ the dunghill Golgotha
A paradise was made.

FROM A HYMN OF HEAVENLY LOVE.

EDMUND SPENSER.

So that next offspring of the Maker's love,
Next to Himselfe in glorious degree,
Degendering to hate, fell from above
Through pride (for pride and love may ill agree,)
And now of sinne to all ensample bee:
How then can sinnful flesh itselfe assure,
Sith purest angels fell to be impure?

But that Eternall Fount of love and grace,
Still flowing forth His goodnesse unto all,
Now seeing left a waste and emptie place
In His wyde pallace, through those angels' fall,
A new unknowen colony therein,
Whose root from earth's base groundworke should begin.

Therefore of clay, base, vile, and next to nought,
Yet form'd by wondrous skill, and by His might
According to an heavenly patterne wrought,
Which He had fashion'd in His wise foresight,
He man did make, and breathed a living spright
Into his face, most beautifull and fayre,
Endewd with wisedome's riches, heavenly, rare.

Such He him made that he resemble might
Himselfe, as mortall thing immortall could;
Him to be lord of every living wight
He made by Love out of his owne like mould,
In whom He might His mightie selfe behould:

T

For Love doth love the thing beloved to see,
That like it selfe in lovely shape may bee.

But man, forgetfull of his Maker's grace
No lesse than Angels' whom he did ensew,
Fell from the hope of promist heavenly place
Into the mouth of Death, to sinners dew,
And all his offspring into thraldome threw,
Where they for ever should in bonds remaine
Of never-dead yet ever-dyeing paine:

Till that great Lord of Love, which him at first
Made of meere love, and after liked well
Seeing him lie like creature long accurst
In that deep horror of despeyred hell,
Him, wretch, in doole would let no longer dwell,
But cast out of that bondage to redeeme,
And pay the price, all were his debt extreme.

Out of the bosome of eternall blisse,
In which He reigned with His glorious Syre,
He downe descended, like a most demisse
And abject thrall, in fleshes fraile attyre,
That He for him might pay sinne's deadly hyre,
And him restore unto that happie state
In which he stood before his haplesse fate.

In flesh at first the guilt committed was,
Therefore in flesh it must be satisfyde;
Nor spirit nor angel, though they man surpas,
Could make amends to God for man's mis-guyde,
But onely man himselfe, who selfe did slyde:
So taking flesh of sacred virgin's wombe,
For man's deare sake He did a man become.

And that most blessed bodie, which was borne
Without all blemish or reprochfull blame,

He freely gave to be both rent and torne
Of cruell hands, who with despightfull shame
Reviling Him, that them most vile became,
At length Him nayled on a gallow-tree,
And slew the iust by most uniust decree.

O huge and most unspeakeable impression
Of Love's deep wound that pierst the piteous hart
Of that deare Lord with so entyre affection,
And, sharply launcing every inner part,
Dolours of death into his soule did dart,
Doing Him die that never it deserved,
To free His foes, that from His heast had swerved!

What hart can feel least touch of so sore launch,
Or thought can think the depth of so deare wound,
Whose bleeding sourse their streames yet never staunch,
But stil do flow, and freshly still redownd,
To heale the sores of sinfull soules unsound,
And cleanse the guilt of that infected cryme
Which was enrooted in all fleshly slyme?

O blessed Well of Love! O Floure of Grace!
O glorious Morning Starre! O Lampe of Light!
Most lively image of Thy Father's face,
Eternal King of Glorie, Lord of might,
Meeke Lambe of God, before all worlds behight,
How can we Thee requite for all this good,
Or what can prize that Thy most precious blood?

Yet nought Thou ask'st in lieu of all this love,
But love of us, for guerdon of Thy paine:
Ay me! what can us lesse than that behove?
Had He required life for us againe,
Had it beene wrong to ask His owne with gaine?
He gave us life, He it restored lost;
Then life were least, that us so little cost.

But He our life hath left unto us free ;
Free that was thrall, and blessed that was band ;
Ne ought demaunds but that we loving bee,
As He Himselfe hath lov'd us afore-hand,
And bound thereto with an eternall band,
Him first to love that was so dearely bought,
And next our brethren, to His image wrought.

Him first to love great right and reason is,
Who first to us our life and being gave,
And after, when we fared had amisse,
Us wretches from the second death did save ;
And last, the food of life, which now we have,
Even He Himselfe in His dear sacrament,
To feede our hungry soules, unto us lent.

Then next, to love our brethren, that were made
Of that selfe mould, and that selfe Maker's hand,
That we, and to the same againe shall fade,
Where they shall have like heritage of land,
However here on higher steps we stand,
Which also were with selfe-same price redeem'd
That we, however of us light esteem'd.

And were they not, yet since that loving Lord
Commanded us to love them for His sake,
Even for His sake, and for His sacred word,
Which in His last bequest He to us spake,
We should them love, and with their needs partake ;
Knowing that whatsoe'er to them we give,
We give to Him by whom we all doe live.

Such mercy He by His most holy reede
Unto us taught, and to approve it trew,
Ensampled it by His most righteous deede,
Shewing us mercie (miserable crew !)

That we the like should to the wretches shew,
And love our brethren; thereby to approve
How much Himselfe that loved us we love.

Then rouze thyself, O Earth! out of thy soyle,
In which thou wallowest like to filthy swyne,
And dost thy mynd in durty pleasures moyle,
Unmindfull of that dearest Lord of thyne;
Lift up to Him thy heavy clouded eyne,
That thou this soveraine bountie mayst beholde,
And read, through Love, His mercies manifold.

Beginne from first, where He encradled was
In simple cratch, wrapt in a wad of hay
Betweene the toylfull oxe and humble asse,
And in what rags, and in how base array,
The glory of our heavenly riches lay,
When Him the silly shepheards came to see,
Whom greatest princes sought on lowest knee.

From thence reade on the storie of His life,
His humble carriage, His unfaulty wayes,
His cancred foes, His fights, His toyle, His strife,
His paines, His povertie, His sharpe assayes,
Through which He past His miserable dayes,
Offending none, and doing good to all,
Yet being malist both by great and small.

And look at last, how of most wretched wights
He taken was, betrayed, and false accused;
How with most scornful taunts and fell despights
He was revyld, disgrast, and foule abused;
How scourgd, how crownd, how buffeted, how brused;
And lastly, how twixt robbers crucifyde
With bitter wounds through hands, through feet and syde.

Then let thy flinty hart that feeles no paine
Empierced be with pittifull remorse,

And let thy bowels bleede in every vaine
At sight of His most sacred heavenly corse,
So torne and mangled with malicious force ;
And let thy soule, whose sins His sorrows wrought,
Melt into tears, and grone in grieved thought.

With sense whereof, whilest so thy soften'd spirit
Is inly toucht, and humbled with meeke zeal
Through meditation of His endlesse merit,
Lift up thy mind to th' Author of thy weale,
And to his soveraine mercie doe appeale :
Learne Him to love that loved thee so deare,
And in thy brest His blessed image beare.

With all thy hart, with all thy soule and minde,
Thou must Him love, and His beheasts embrace :
All other loves, with which the world doth blind
Weake fancies, and stir up affectiones base,
Thou must renounce and utterly displace ;
And give thyself unto Him full and free,
That full and freely gave Himselfe to thee.

Then shalt thou feele thy spirit so possest
And ravisht with devouring great desire
Of His dear selfe, that shall thy feeble brest
Inflame with love, and set thee all on fire
With burning zeale, through every part entire,
That in no earthly thing thou shalt delight,
But in His sweet and amiable sight.

Thenceforth all world's desire will in thee dye ;
And all earth's glorie, on which men do gaze,
Seeme durt and drosse in thy pure-sighted eye,
Compar'd to that celestiall beautie's blaze,
Whose glorious beames all fleshly sense doth daze
With admiration of their passing light,
Blinding the eyes, and lumining the spright.

Then shall thy ravisht soul inspired bee
With heavenly thoughts, farre above humane skil,
And thy bright radiant eyes shall plainly see
Th' idee of His pure glorie present still
Before thy face, that all thy spirits shall fill
With sweete enragement of celestiall love,
Kindled through sight of those faire things above.

PSALM XXIII.

SIR PHILIP SIDNEY.

The Lord, the Lord my shepheard is,
   And so can never I
     Tast missery.
He rests me in greene pastures his;
   By waters still and sweete
     He guides my feete.

Hee me revives; leades me the way
   Which righteousnesse doth take,
     For His name sake.
Yea, though I should through valleys stray
   Of death's dark shade, I will
     Noe whitt feare ill.

For Thou, deere Lord, Thou me besett'st,
   Thy rodd and Thy staff be
     To comfort me:
Before me Thou a table sett'st,
   Even when foes' envious eye
     Doth it espy.

Thou oil'st my head, Thou fill'st my cupp;
   Nay, more, Thou endless Good,
     Shalt give me food.

To Thee, I say, ascended up,
　Where Thou, the Lord of all,
　　Dost hold Thy hall.

MY PILGRIMAGE.

SIR WALTER RALEIGH.

Give me my scallop-shell of quiet,
My staff of faith to walk upon,
My scrip of ioye, (immortal diet!)
My bottle of saluation,
My gowne of glory, hope's true gage:
And thus I take my pilgrimage.

Blood must be my body's balmer,
While my soule, like peaceful palmer,
Travelleth towards the land of heauen:
Other balm will not be giuen.
Over the silver mountains,
Where spring the nectar fountains,
　　There will I kiss
　　The bowl of bliss,
And drink mine everlasting fill
Upon euery milken hill:
My soul will be adry before,
But after that will thirst no more.

　*　　*　　*　　*　　*

PRAYER.

GEORGE HERBERT.

Of what an easy, quick access,
My blessed Lord, art Thou! how suddenly
　May our requests Thy ear invade!
To shew that state dislikes not easiness,
If I but lift mine eyes, my suit is made:
Thou canst no more not hear than Thou canst die.

    Of what supreme almighty power
Is Thy great arm, which spans the east and west,
    And tacks the centre to the sphere !
By it do all things live their measured hour :
We cannot ask the thing which is not there,
Blaming the shallowness of our request.

    Of what immeasurable love
Art Thou possess'd, who, when Thou couldst not die,
    Wert fain to take our flesh and curse,
And for our sakes in person sin reprove ;
That by destroying that which tied Thy purse,
Thou might'st make way for liberality !

    Since, then, these three wait on Thy throne,
Ease, Power, and Love, I value Prayer so,
    That were I to leave all but one,
Wealth, fame, endowments, virtues, all should go :
I and dear Prayer would together dwell,
And quickly gain, for each inch lost, an ell.

ON THE PROVIDENCE OF GOD.

RICHARD BAXTER.

  My Lord hath taught me how to want
    A place wherein to put my head :
  While He is mine, I'll be content
    To beg or lack my daily bread.

  Heaven is my roof, earth is my floor ;
    Thy love can keep me dry and warm :
  Christ and Thy bounty are my store,
    Thy angels guard me from all harm.

  Must I forsake the soil and air
    Where first I drew my vital breath ?

> That way may be as near and fair
> Thence I may come to Thee by death.
>
> All countries are my Father's lands:
> Thy Sun, Thy Love, doth shine on all;
> We may in all lift up pure hands,
> And with acceptance on Thee call.
>
> What if in prison I must dwell,
> May I not there converse with Thee?
> Save me from sin, Thy wrath, and hell,
> Call me Thy child, and I am free.
>
> No walls or bars can keep Thee out,
> None can confine a holy soul;
> The streets of Heaven it walks about,
> None can its liberty control.

But it would be impossible to close this brief sketch of English Hymnology without speaking of the marvellous burst of sacred song which has filled the land during the forty years since this book was first written. Fifty years ago Tate and Brady reigned supreme in all our ordinary parish churches except those touched by the Evangelical Revival of the commencement of the century. Now probably not a Church is without its hymn-book culled from all ages and sources. The number of new writers is as remarkable as the number of hymns. To begin with, Keble's "Christian Year" of itself opened a new epoch. Far and wide as the English-speaking race, its silver tones have penetrated, sung in every English Church throughout the world, lisped at the mother's knee in every home. If we examine the list of authors in all the

Hymnals we find that more than half belong to the latter half of this century; clergymen and laymen, literary men and simple souls whose inspiration was the faith that made them seers, are among them, and many women. To grasp the range of the singers we need only name a few of those best known—Keble, Lyte, Bishops Bickersteth, Wordsworth, and Walsham How, Dean Alford, Cardinal Newman, Father Faber, Monsell, Sabine Baring Gould, S. J. Stone, Horatius Bonar; Harriet Beecher Stowe, Adelaide Procter, Christina Rossetti, Frances Alexander, Frances Ridley Havergal, Charlotte Elliott, Caroline Noel, Elizabeth Clephane (Author of " The Ninety and Nine ").

The subjects are as varied as the writers, hymns for festivals and for all hours and seasons, hymns Eucharistic, Baptismal, Marriage and Funeral, hymns for Missions, Home and Foreign, tender and joyous songs for the children. Everything speaks of life and movement of united service and worship. These forty years have certainly not been a period of tranquillity or sleepy agreement. Differences have been forcibly emphasized on all sides and fearlessly carried out in many instances to their extreme logical consequences, ecclesiastical or non-ecclesiastical. No one can say it has been a time of mild and colourless Undenominationalism. Yet from the farthest North of Presbyterian Scotland to the Land's End you may hear sung by surpliced choirs or Highland congregations Sabine Baring Gould's "Through the night of doubt and sorrow" or Horatius Bonar's "I was a wandering sheep." From the farthest East (in Neale's "translations"), from the farthest West of "Revivalist America" their voices come. In all the hymn-books there is of course a considerable margin not approved by all, but in all the hymn-books the great majority are loved and used by all. If at any time we feel desponding as to retrograde ebbs or undermining encroachments, as to the lowering of Christian life, or breaches of Christian unity, perhaps there is not a better tonic, than to read over the subjects of the hymns and the names of the hymn-writers in any of our popular hymn-books, to rejoice in the unity of the singers, and to lift up our hearts in the great harmony of the songs.

CHAPTER XII

CONCLUSION

E have been listening to the murmurs of the great stream of sacred song as it has flowed on from age to age; sometimes nearly buried in the sands of time, sometimes parted into many smaller streams; now bursting barriers of centuries in a rush of music, and then flowing calmly in a broader current, but never utterly dried up or silent. Never has the ceaseless song of Nature to her Maker been altogether without words; and the music of the Creature has never been wholly unaccompanied by the hymn of the Child. The new song of the redeemed hushed the first discords of the Fall, and met the echoes of the earlier song of unfallen creatures ere they were quite lost inside the closed gates of Eden. Ever the same, it has yet been ever new. It has been no languid, luxurious strain, floating over a banquet. Like the old song of Moses, it has been throughout a battle-song; a chant, indeed, of victory and redemption, but sung by pilgrims and soldiers who had yet a wilderness to cross ere they reached the

land of promise and the city of God. From the day when Mary the mother of Jesus sang the first Christian hymn, to the latest that has entered our modern hymn-books, One Name, which is above every name, has made all its music. Ephrem, the Syrian monk, sang his psalms of welcome where once the children of Jerusalem had strewed their palm branches; Gregory of Nazianzum, poor, old, and lonely, found Him fatherland and home; Ambrose filled Milan with the praises of the Redeemer of the nations, the Sun of righteousness; Prudentius sang how the dead reposed in Him; Bernard rejoiced in His cross and His promise; Luther called on all Christian people to triumph in his completed redemption; Wesley fled to Him while the tempest still was high;[1] Cowper pointed to the Fountain which could wash all stains away. All sang as of a victory already won, and yet as themselves still in the battle-field, and pressing onward to the prize. They sang of a Sun which had arisen, and yet, as travellers at night, of a Day which had yet to dawn. They sang of Redemption already accomplished, but also of a City yet to come. And the Sun whose light they knew, yet waited for, the Victor and Redeemer, the Captain in the present warfare, the Joy and Glory of the heavenly city, are all One. All along

---

[1] There is a lovely legend of the origin of the hymn "Jesus, lover of my soul." It is said that Charles Wesley was standing at the open window of his house in Marylebone, looking out on a storm which was breaking over the heights of Hampstead, when a frightened little bird flew to his breast for refuge from the pursuit of a hawk, and the words came to him,

"Let me to Thy bosom fly,
Till the storm of life is past."

the ages, through all the tumult of the world, and all the wanderings of the Church, that song has never paused. The joyful " Thou wast slain, and hast redeemed us to God by Thy blood," of those who have overcome, has never been without its echo from the struggling multitudes on the battle-field below. Nor is it pausing now. Mercies, new every morning, are still calling forth new songs of praise.[1]

> " To every freshly opening flower
> Fresh songs of joy are due ;
> For whilst time flies and comes no more,
> The seasons bloom anew." [2]

The snow-drops of this spring are as pure and fresh as they were when the world was young. The birds welcomed the sunrise this morning with as keen a joy as they did when first he dawned on Eden. Infant life is as fresh to-day as when the first child earth ever saw played at the feet of Eve ; and spiritual life is as fresh to-day as when Enoch walked with God. Nature never grows old ; the youth of the Church of God is as unfading as that of the angels at the sepulchre, the " young men " in shining garments, who had shouted for joy at the creation ; and as the Church is, so is each of her members. The good tidings strike with as fresh a joy on the heart of him who believes them first to-day as they did on the shepherds from the lips of

---

[1] Largely proved by the tide of new Christian song which has enriched our hymn-books during the forty years since this book was written.

[2] Goethe.

angels, or on St. Paul from the voice of Jesus. And therefore the great matin hymn still rises ever new from earth to heaven.

How many sweet and joyous, or deep and touching hymns are there in our days, as doubtless there have been in all times, which never reach beyond the little family or social circle which they gladden! How many have been written to comfort one sorrowful heart, and having accomplished that, are heard no more! How many gush out on occasion of some especial sorrow, or joy, or deliverance, and are forgotten like the song of the birds that poured out their happy music yesterday morning!

Yet none of these are lost; they reach God, to whom they are sung, and they speak of Him to man; and more neither song nor singer can seek to be, or to do. And not only this. Doubtless the heavenly City has also its order of singers specially endowed and trained for their work. Yet in this new temple which is silently rising day by day, all the stones are musical when struck by the right Hand; and the richest songs have sometimes been sung by those who sang but one, whose names are lost to us for ever. There are tens of thousands who never wrote a hymn, who may yet have made better spiritual music with many hymns than those who wrote them. The hymn-writer only speaks the thought or feeling of all Christians, and the echo may often be sweeter and purer than the original notes, because less mixed up with self. The faith which sees the Invisible, and is loftier than all flights of imagination, is not the dower of a few, but the heritage of all. The whole Church is a Choir as well as a Priesthood. The harps of God with the priestly robes of festival, and the victors' crowns, are the purchased possession of all who stand by that sea of glass mingled with fire. But what those images mean, and what that song and that joy will be, we know not yet; we only know that it shall be, and that its first notes only are to be learned on earth.

Has there not, moreover, amidst all the din and discord around, been a growing beauty and power in this song? Has there not been a development of Christian doctrine, not independent of the Bible, but evolved out of it? Has not the Church been gradually mounted to the height of the Book, and can we not, in some measure, trace this in her hymns? Is not the atoning power of the death of the Lamb of God more fully brought out in the Ambrosian than in the Oriental hymns? Through the wars and convulsions of the Middle Ages, when the soil of modern society was being formed by the crumbling of old civilizations and the upheaving of new races; through those times of darkness and tumult, when it seemed so often as if the end of all things must be at hand to close the terrible struggle, whilst the apprehension of the " day of wrath " was often so present and vivid, did not the Cross shine more and more clearly as the one refuge from the judgment-throne? And then at the Reformation, when before, since the days of St. Paul, had the world rung with such force and clearness with the tidings of great joy, of Redemption and free forgiveness, of the access of all to the Great High

U

Priest, of the priesthood of all Christians, the sacredness of all vocations, as in the hymns of Germany? Again, when in the eighteenth century Zinzendorf and the Wesleys arose, did not the old message gain something fresh from the old fountain as it issued thence anew? To Luther, the Grand Turk was simply an Antichrist; to Zinzendorf and the evangelical English Christians of the eighteenth century the heathen were part of that lost world which the Son of God came to redeem. To the age of battle for truth succeeded the age of Propagation of the Gospel. The hymn-books of the eighteenth century begin to contain missionary hymns. The grand missionary hymn "The Cross is in the field" leads on the conquering hosts, never to cease till the refrain changes to the triumphant "The Cross has won the field."

And now in our hymns of to-day is there not a fresh joyousness as of new songs of the morning? Does not the gospel of the kingdom, the brotherhood of man, the corporate life of the Church sing out with a fuller volume than before? St. Francis's change of front from the solitudes to the multitudes is not lost; it finds utterance in the Songs of the Church to her Lord, as well as in her labours among men; the trumpet tone of a conquering host is in them, the onward movement of "Christian Soldiers marching on to war" against all wrong and sin, the breath of the corporate life which reaches beyond this visible world of the

> "Church whose one foundation
> Is Jesus Christ her Lord,"

whose responsive choirs embrace the "Humble ones and Holy who rest on high with Him" as well as those who toil and serve below.

Are there not signs of the ethical being more blended with the spiritual in our hymns as with the political in our efforts at reform? Signs that God Himself is felt more and more to be the God of nature and humanity, Source of all science, and Father of all the brotherhood of man, the God who calleth the stars by name, and, also, the sheep; the Infinite who "telleth the number" of the countless suns of the heaven and who "healeth the broken in heart"? And with the deepening and widening of the corporate life has there not come more of the triumph and gladness of the ancient psalms; and yet also at the same time with the divine optimism which aims at the lifting all mankind here and now to the best they can be, has there not grown a more fearless fathoming of the depths of the evils that exist here and now, a "Divine discontent" with things as they are, with our civilization as it is; and through this practical recognition of the worst and struggling for the best is there not arising a new cry for the great Advent of the Christ, Son of man and King of men—a cry not despondent, but full of glorious hope; not damping effort for combating present evils, but inspiring it; not seeking a mere individual escape from sin and sorrow for each through death, but a glorious triumph for all over sin and death, through the risen and conquering Lord? Are there not yet depths in the Gospel of St. John, and heights in the Apocalyptic vision, a fulness of revelation of

Him who is at once the Lamb of God and the Son of man, the Son of God and the Bridegroom of the Church, which the Church is yet slowly travelling up to apprehend?[1] May there not yet even on

[1] "As the one force of the magnet manifests itself at two opposing poles, exactly according to the same law, reappearing in the spiritual world, we have two developments of the same Christian theology, which make themselves felt from the very first, whereof St. Paul may be taken as chief representative of the one and St. John of the other. We cannot do more than trace the distinction in some of its broadest features. We see there St. Paul making man the starting-point of his theology. The divine image in man, that image lost, the impossibility of its restoration by any power of his own; these are the grounds which he first lays—as eminently in his great dogmatic Epistle to the Romans. But St. John, upon the other hand, starts from the opposite point, from the *theology* in the more restricted sense of the word, in this justifying the title ὁ θεολογός, which he bears. His centre and starting-point is the Divine Love, and out of that he unfolds all. Thus we have man delivered in St. Paul, God delivering in St. John; man rising in the one, God stooping in the other, and thus each travels over an hemisphere in the great orb of Christian truth, and they not each singly, but between them, embrace and encircle it all.

"For this is part of the glory of Christ as compared with His servants, as compared with the chiefest of His servants, that He alone stands at the absolute centre of humanity the one completely harmonious man, unfolding all that was in that humanity *equally* upon all sides, fully upon all sides, the only One in whom the real and the ideal met and were absolutely at one. And as it was meant that the Gospel of Christ should embrace all lands, should fix at its first entrance into the world a firm root upon either of its two great cultivated portions, so in these two, in St. Paul and in St. John, we recognize wondrous preparations in the providence of God for the winning to the obedience of the cross both the western and the eastern world. Who can fail to see in the great Apostle of Tarsus, in his discursive intellect, in his keen dialectics, in his philosophic training, the man armed to dispute with Stoic and Epicurean at Athens, who should teach the Church how she should take the West for her inheritance? And in St. John, the full significance of whose writings for the Church is probably yet to be revealed, we have the progenitor of every con-

earth be sung psalms and hymns and spiritual songs, deeper and more heavenly than any earth has ever yet heard? For the Church is not journeying away from the first Advent, but on to the second; nor is she left to dig for herself her treasures of truth out of a Book written in a language dead for centuries. The Book is spoken to her still by a living Voice, the Voice of Him who testifies of Jesus.

The song of redemption is no mere echo of an earlier song pealing in fainter and fainter cadence from age to age. It is the rebound of the living waters ever freshly flowing from heaven to earth; and if anything of echo mingles with it, it is the reverberation of a song which is drawing nearer and nearer, the song of the great multitude which no man can number, which is to burst on earth in the Day which is approaching. For there is a Triumphal Entry to come; the gates of the heavenly City shall yet open wide, and the multitude from within shall meet the throng coming up from the Jordan and the wilderness, and both shall form one adoring company round Him who cometh no more in humiliation, but mighty to save. No cross shall follow that day of triumph! those songs shall never again fall into discord, nor be quenched in tears: and in the temple in which that procession shall close, the City which is our Temple, there shall be no Pharisees, nor traffickers to be expelled, and no blind or lame to be healed. The new Ideal City shall be

---

templative spirit that has delighted to sink and to lose itself, and in the sense of its own littleness in the brightness and in the glory of God."—ARCHBISHOP TRENCH's *Hulsean Lectures*.

filled with the new song, and the gates of the City shall be open night and day; and there shall be no night there. All that is symbolized by light, and all that is only to be uttered by song, shall pour forth through those gates for ever, for the healing and the joy of all.

THE END.

Richard Clay & Sons, Limited, London & Bungay.

WORKS BY THE LATE
MRS. RUNDLE CHARLES.

THREE MARTYRS OF THE NINETEENTH CENTURY.
Studies from the Lives of Livingstone, Gordon, and Patteson. Crown 8vo, cloth boards, 3s. 6d.

MARTYRS AND SAINTS OF THE FIRST TWELVE CENTURIES.
Studies from the Lives of the Black-Letter Saints of the English Calendar. Crown 8vo, cloth boards, 5s.

SKETCHES OF THE WOMEN OF CHRISTENDOM.
Crown 8vo, cloth boards, 3s. 6d.

AGAINST THE STREAM.
The Story of an Heroic Age in England. With illustrations. Crown 8vo, cloth boards, 4s.

CONQUERING AND TO CONQUER.
A Story of Rome in the days of St. Jerome. Crown 8vo, cloth boards, 2s. 6d.

LAPSED, BUT NOT LOST.
A Story of Roman Carthage. Crown 8vo, cloth bds., 2s. 6d.

THOUGHTS AND CHARACTERS.
Being Selections from the Writings of the same Author. Crown 8vo, cloth boards, 3s. 6d.

ECCE ANCILLA DOMINI. MARY THE MOTHER OF OUR LORD.
Studies in the Ideal of Womanhood. Post 8vo, cloth, 2s.

ECCE HOMO, ECCE REX.
Pages from the Story of the Moral Conquests of Christianity. Post 8vo, cloth boards, 3s. 6d.

THE BEATITUDES.
Thoughts for all Saints' Day. Post 8vo, cloth bds., 1s. 6d.

"BY THE MYSTERY OF THY HOLY INCARNATION."
Post 8vo, cloth boards, 1s. 6d.

By the late MRS. RUNDLE CHARLES—Continued.

"BY THY CROSS AND PASSION."
Thoughts on the Words spoken around and on the Cross. Post 8vo, cloth boards, 1s. 6d.

"BY THY GLORIOUS RESURRECTION AND ASCENSION."
Easter Thoughts. Post 8vo, cloth boards, 1s. 6d.

"BY THE COMING OF THE HOLY GHOST."
Thoughts for Whitsuntide. Post 8vo, cloth boards, 1s. 6d.

THE TRUE VINE.
Post 8vo, cloth boards, 1s. 6d.

THE GREAT PRAYER OF CHRISTENDOM.
Thoughts on the Lord's Prayer. Post 8vo, cloth boards, 1s. 6d.

WITHIN THE VEIL.
Studies in the Epistle to the Hebrews. Post 8vo, cloth boards, 1s. 6d.

THE BOOK OF THE UNVEILING.
Studies in the Revelation of St. John the Divine. Post 8vo, cloth boards, 1s. 6d.

AN OLD STORY OF BETHLEHEM.
One Link in the Great Pedigree. Fcap. 4to, with Six Plates beautifully printed in colours. Cloth boards, 2s. 6d.

JOAN THE MAID.
Deliverer of England and France. Demy 8vo, cloth boards, 3s. 6d.

SONGS, OLD AND NEW.
Demy 16mo, cloth boards, 3s.

EARLY CHRISTIAN MISSIONS OF IRELAND, SCOTLAND, AND ENGLAND.
Crown 8vo, cloth boards, 4s.

LADY AUGUSTA STANLEY.
Reminiscences. 18mo, limp cloth, 6d.

ATTILA AND HIS CONQUERORS.
A Story of the Days of St. Patrick and St. Leo the Great. Crown 8vo, cloth boards, 3s. 6d.

SOCIETY FOR PROMOTING CHRISTIAN KNOWLEDGE,
LONDON: NORTHUMBERLAND AVENUE, W.C.

www.ingramcontent.com/pod-product-compliance
Lightning Source LLC
Chambersburg PA
CBHW022054230426
43672CB00008B/1172